BITTERSWEET

A Memoir

Introduction

Climbing mountains exhilarates me. The challenge, exertion, endurance, and stretched muscles trigger a rush of emotion. Experience proves I can't climb alone. I need stronger ones than me by my side.

Life-changing climbs include Jiuhua in China, a Himalayan peak in Nepal, Angkor Wat in Cambodia, Petra in Jordan, Machu Picchu in Peru, and Christ the Redeemer in Brazil. The view is dramatically broader from the top. But I can't live on the summit. I must go down eventually. And climbing mountains is bittersweet. The sweat is disgustingly bitter; meeting the challenge is incredibly sweet.

The ground is not always level, and I may not be sure-footed. There are times I slip down into a grimy pit. It's hard to pull myself up and it takes as much energy and determination as climbing a mountain. Pit dwelling discourages rather than exhilarates me. Again, I need stronger ones than me to help me claw my way out.

And then there's the wilderness, often called a desert. Though it rarely requires climbing, the wilderness is a lonely and desolate place. A wilderness may be frigid like the Arctic or Antarctic, or at times swelteringly hot like the Sahara. Both are inhospitable. When I'm in the wilderness, I walk forever and wonder if I've accomplished anything or grown in even a small way. Each day is like the last and seemingly endless. I need stronger ones than me in the wilderness.

Mountains, pits, and wilderness seasons are multi-faceted. They may be exquisite and life-threatening simultaneously. God is present, but on most occasions waits to be invited to participate. They provide opportunity to reflect on internal and external battles amid prayers for relief. These seasons are not only natural but spiritual, with giants to slay along the way. Sweat, endurance, and faith are required to conquer them. I relax and enjoy the view on a mountain top, occasionally oblivious to dangers lurking nearby. Other times, I falter in the downward journey. Our spiritual enemies wait for opportunities to attack.

I need stronger ones than me at every level. I need family, friends, and mentors, but more than people, I need the fullness of the Godhead—Father, Son, and Holy Spirit. Pride says, "I can do it myself." Humility says, "Jesus, help me! Give me wisdom, speak to me, send some warriors to pray and lift my arms." God-given purpose fulfillment depends on God, but also my determination and action to see it through to its perfect end. God's purposes are never thwarted, but if we don't engage, He may choose someone else.

I attended a women's conference in the spring of 1996, where the theme centered on the story of Caleb, one of the twelve Israelites Moses sent to spy out the promised land. He and Joshua were the only two spies who came back with a good report. Caleb believed that through God the Israelites could overcome the giants standing in their way, and they could take the land God had promised to Abraham and his descendants. Caleb was obedient, courageous, and committed to seeing the fulfillment of the promise. Later, after forty years of wandering in the wilderness, Caleb declared that his strength at eighty-five was just as it had been at forty-five. God had promised the mountain of Hebron to him years before, and it was time to take the mountain (Joshua 14:6–15). He believed God until the promise was fulfilled.

The Bible teacher said, "Who is called to be a Caleb?"

I immediately responded, along with a handful of other women.

Turning to me, she said, "You ask when is it your turn? The time is now! I had to do some cutting away."

I was nearing my forty-fifth birthday and had not considered what my future might be forty years later. I pivoted from that day. Mountaintops, pits, and wilderness experiences are always part of life, but the conference speaker challenged me to climb my mountain. I accepted the challenge more than thirty years ago and have not looked back.

PART ONE.
IMPOSSIBILITIES

Chapter One

Dynamic Shifts

The road from Ordinary, Virginia to Uncertain, Texas was a mixture of exhilaration and pure terror. Jeff, my 14-year-old son and I drove off in a car past its prime toward an unpredictable future. But at forty-five years old, I, too, was past my prime. If I could make it, surely the car would? After hugs and prayers from friends, we waved goodbye to the small town of Ordinary, Virginia and set off before the sun set.

I thought, *Today won't be so bad. We only need to get to North Carolina.* Jeff followed the map while I kept my eyes on the road, my mind racing with *what if's*. But no matter. We were on our way.

My resolution and sense of peace staggered when the temperature gauge on the car ran hot. It was dark, now traveling on narrow country roads without streetlights. I pulled over, and Jeff and I looked at each other. What do we do now? One of my greatest fears is car trouble. Jeff got out of the car and lifted the hood, as steam filled the air amidst the hissing sound of boiling fluids. After some time, Jeff took a rag and opened the radiator cap. We had water, so he cautiously poured it into the reservoir. *What have I done?* I thought. *Was that really You, God? Are the giants waiting for me greater than my faith can handle? What happens now?*

It was a gut-wrenching step to leave my church and friends in Virginia. I was unnerved when the car overheated, and I needed to find my feet. I remembered the Scripture Habakkuk 3:19: "The Sovereign Lord is my strength; He makes my feet like the feet of a deer; He enables me to tread on the heights." We resumed our journey after the radiator cooled, convinced that faith would prevail over fear.

Dream fulfillment intersects high and low points in our lives. The "divine appointment" connects the dream with events already in process. In my case, fascination with cultures, painful life experiences, decades of medical and mental health education, faith, and a call to bring healing to people globally intertwined months before the road trip. I entered a thrilling yet challenging way of life and purpose, amazed God chose me as His handmaiden. Long-term missions began when Don Stephens, founder of Mercy Ships, shared a life-changing message at my church in the spring of 1996.

The *Caribbean Mercy* (one of Mercy Ships' vessels) came to the coast near Ordinary, Virginia on a public relations tour. Don spoke at LightHouse Church to an eager and attentive congregation. Excitement filled the room, yet not a sound was heard as we waited for this spiritual giant to share a dynamic message. Everything Don said seemed directed toward me. I know God spoke to many people, but I also knew to pay attention. Don said, "We need to forget what happened in the past … We can't change the past, but we can change the future … There is much work to be done in missions."

I felt the familiar stirring deep in my spirit I had experienced as a young child during messages on missions. I wanted to respond but hesitated. I had visited the *Anastasis*, Mercy Ships' flagship two years earlier, in 1994. Convinced this was where I belonged, I asked crew members how I might join, but learned there were no positions for psychologists, and single parents with children were not allowed to serve on the ships. My hopes were shattered as I already felt the tug toward missions. *Would the response be different now?* I feared another rejection. I'd had a lifetime of rejection. Yet I knew if I did not speak with Don, it would be disobedience. Equally important, the opportunity would be lost. It was now or never.

I went forward, my heart pounding. When Don finished talking with others I said, "Would you be able to use a psychologist?" Don was quiet, the silence deafening as I waited. He then reached in his pocket for a business card, but there were none left. Taking out his used boarding pass, Don wrote a name and phone number on it. He said, "Call this man." Hope stirred when I considered there might be a place for me after all.

The realization that past experiences and present circumstances would not limit God's plans for my life dumbfounded me. Trauma perpetrated by others and my resultant poor choices made me question if God would call me to follow Him to the uttermost parts of the earth as He called missionary heroes in the books I read. Moving into long-term missions was a giant leap from joining short-term mission trips, counseling locally in private practice and serving as a volunteer counselor at LightHouse. And being a single parent was not only my primary responsibility but also a privilege. Putting God first, family second, ministry third was not to be compromised. Don's message confirmed these priorities as God-ordained.

Mercy Ships' stories demonstrate to me that seemingly impossible dreams are realized through faith, determination, hard work, and a willingness to surrender everything to God who holds our lives in His hands. An often-told story recounts how God answered prayer in a miraculous way. More than forty years ago, the crew worked on the newly acquired ship for three years, with one hour of power per day. They waited with anticipation for the *Anastasis* to sail from Greece to bring hope and healing to the world's poor. They prayed to see God's kingdom come. They wanted to be fishers of men.

The crew spent hours in prayer with times of retreat on the beach. They did not pray for fish; they prayed for God to move. God did move, but not in the way these volunteers expected. First one fish, then another, then another jumped on the shore from the ocean. They kept jumping, and 8,301 fish landed on the beach.

The cook on board was Norwegian—skilled in the art of preparing fish. Deyon Stephens, the co-founder of Mercy Ships, told how the crew carried, cleaned, and then ate those fish for months. She reminds us that miracles take a lot of work. Walking out the dream takes grit.

I, too, have miracle stories which encourage me in particularly difficult times. After I read the book *Daring to Live on The Edge*, my paying clients left, and those who continued counseling had little funds. I struggled to buy food, and my faith wavered. A friend came to the door with a cooler filled to the brim with fish. God provided an overabundance of fish, and at the same time confirmed His call for me to be a fisher of men, just like the staff and crew of Mercy Ships.

Soon after, I needed to move due to lack of funds, so my son and I stayed with friends who owned a farm. Jeff graduated from eighth grade, and I wanted to make him a cake. I had cake mix but no money for fuel to go buy eggs. I cried silently and prayed for God to intervene.

Then I walked into the kitchen and saw three eggs on the counter. "Where did these eggs come from?" I asked.

The father said, "Jeff collected them a little while ago."

I said, "I can't believe it. It's a miracle. I needed three eggs to make this cake."

"It's not a miracle there are eggs," The father replied, "It is a miracle there are three. We only get two eggs from our chickens."

Whether the chickens laying three eggs is a miracle may be debated. But with my simple, heartfelt and desperate prayer, Father God heard my prayer and created the eggs I needed to make a cake for Jeff. He created life for me to share love with someone else. That's what He does. All the time.

The fish and the eggs prompted deeper reflection, and I sat in God's presence in an attitude of prayer. He gave me so much and I gave Him so little. I realized everything I owned was a gift from God, most items given through people He put in my life. I thought, *what do I have to give you, God?* An old hymn came to mind as I sat quietly before Him.

> *Vainly we offer each ample oblation,*
> *Vainly with gifts would his favor secure;*
> *Richer by far is the heart's adoration,*
> *Dearer to God are the prayers of the poor.*[1]

People can't give anything tangible and of our own making to God. He owns everything and He's the giver of good gifts. Mercy Ships crew, dreaming of how to make Him known on the earth, and a single mother with fledgling faith, bless the Father by giving their heart and their prayers. He receives from us when we walk in faith, and He becomes our first love.

The gateway between stubborn obstacles and dream fulfillment is faith. God's purposes are not thwarted, and without a vision the people perish. Faith is the catalyst for movement. Faith is the substance of things hoped for; the evidence of things not seen. Faith energizes promises of the kingdom to be appropriated and manifested on earth.

Chapter Two

A Riot of Color in a Dreary Grey World

The time had come to step out in faith. What seemed an abrupt change in direction was in process from before the foundations of the world. The combination of life experiences and completing five degrees would put me just where God wanted me to bring healing to suffering people globally.

Professional preparation began with a hospital diploma in nursing, followed by a bachelor's degree in psychology, a second bachelor's in nursing, a master of psychiatric nursing, and a Ph.D. in industrial and organizational psychology.

As a pre-teen, I wrote an autobiography declaring I wanted to be a nurse but not work with psychiatric patients because they scared me. The paradigm shift occurred on a typical day on a medical-surgical hospital unit where I was responsible for forty patients and a few workers. Three life-threatening incidents happened within 15 minutes, and they required triage. The sudden heart attack took priority, followed by the person complaining of chest pain. But what haunted me was the woman bleeding internally who asked, with terror in her eyes, "Am I going to die?" I had no time to sit with her, not only because of the two emergencies, but also because there were thirty-seven more people in my care. Her words, her voice, her eyes lingered in my thoughts and in my heart. Within three years, I moved from general and intensive care to psychiatric nursing.

About ten years later, I sensed another transition. Providing psychiatric care was meaningful, but making organizations healthier was equally important to me. I completed a doctorate in industrial and organizational psychology to blend both worlds. I loved training others in addition to providing direct care myself. Individual counseling helps one, but training others builds capacity.

The same is true in the church. Evangelism helps one, but training the one and others grows the kingdom exponentially. I hoped to blend mental health care, training, and working in organizations with planting spiritual seeds. But where would I start? Jesus is the Rock, the foundation, and unless the Lord builds the house, the house won't stand. I reflected on my early life, spiritual roots, and complicated surrender to Jesus.

Near north Chicago was my home, and I was born after midnight on December 13th in the dead of winter. The temperature, a chilling 11 degrees Fahrenheit, discouraged unnecessary outside activities. Five inches of impenetrable snow covered the cement sidewalk like a blanket. I imagine my pregnant mother braving the storm, as she steadied herself on the steps to avoid a fall on the way to the hospital. Few people had cars in 1950. I wonder if my parents owned one or if they waited for a ride in the freezing cold.

December 13th is a Swedish holiday (Santa Lucia Day) honoring St. Lucia, an Italian martyr of the fourth century. Though I'm not Catholic, I love learning about past heroes of faith, and I've connected to St. Lucia in a special way since most of my ancestors are Swedish. In the Swedish tradition, St. Lucia is the bearer of light during the long Swedish winters. December 13th was considered the longest day of the year in the old almanac. It was a dangerous night. Legends declared supernatural beings were abroad and all animals could speak. Some accounts and Catholic resources describe Lucia as a 20-year-old Catholic Sicilian girl who was martyred by the Romans for her faith in the year 304 AD. Lucia's mother arranged a marriage for her with a pagan man, but Lucia refused, devoted to her faith. She convinced her mother Christ was a better life partner, but the angry suitor went to the Roman authorities and sentenced Lucia to become a prostitute in a brothel. Divine intervention prevented her from being physically carried away. Undaunted, the soldiers lit a fire around her. Yet the flames did not touch her. Lucia died on December 13th, stabbed through the neck with a sword. St. Lucia remained faithful to Jesus throughout trials, temptations, persecution, and a horrific death.

The Prayer to St. Lucia reads:

> Saint Lucy, you did not hide your light under a basket, but let it shine for the whole world, for all the centuries to see. We may not suffer torture in our lives the way you did, but we are still called to let the light of our Christianity illumine our daily lives. Please help us to have the courage to bring our Christianity into our work, our recreation, our relationships, and our conversation—every corner of our day. Amen.

St. Lucia remains a role model for me, and exemplifies a Scripture I live by:

> Then I heard a loud voice in heaven say: "Now have come the salvation and the power and the kingdom of our God, and the authority of his Messiah. For the accuser of our brothers and sisters, who accuses them before our God day and night, has been hurled down. They triumphed over him by the blood of the Lamb and by the word of their testimony; they did not love their lives so much as to shrink from death." (Revelation 12:10-12)

Further, she represents Jesus, who is the light of the world, pierced by a sword on the cross as He died in our place for the sins of the world. Through Jesus, the power lies not in the enemy's weapon, but in the sword of the Spirit of God.

I attended a Lutheran church as a young child, consistent with my Swedish heritage. I listened intently as missionaries told stories and shared their experiences through 8mm reels of film projected on the wall. The words, the images, activated my senses and my heart. Footage of African children being given life-saving vaccines and the story of Jesus being shared in towns and villages drew me in. I desperately wanted to go. I wanted to travel to exotic places and meet people who live differently. I wondered if missions might be in my future.

I enjoyed going to St. Luke's Lutheran Church, a historic stone building sandwiched between houses in an old Chicago neighborhood. The structure itself was vibrant, with a magnificent, vaulted ceiling, stained glass windows, and row upon row of symmetrical pews. The pipe organ billowed out hymns with melodious voices permeating the building. Sundays blessed me with the gift of peace. "Lamb of God, who takes away the sins of the world, hear our prayer. Lamb of God, who takes away the sins of the world, have mercy on us." I loved the liturgy. I didn't quite understand it, but it stirred me.

The church was a sanctuary; not only because it was a majestic, magnificent spiritual space, but because it calmed my mind, my body, my emotions, and my spirit. I prayed and trusted God knew best and would see me through. Though the sermons often seemed to go on forever and I missed much of what was said, I enjoyed the harmony and peace I found as I lingered on the pew.

On occasion, I attended other churches during my childhood, and the exquisite stained-glass windows told stories of agony and ecstasy of the life of Jesus. The bitter and the sweet. I often reflect on a scene from the movie *A Knight's Tale.*

William: "You favor Cathedrals."

Jocelyn: "I come for confession and the glass—a riot of color in a dreary grey world."

"A riot of color in a dreary grey world" paints a picture of my childhood.

Our apartment complex had a cement back yard and a grey, wooden fence. In summer, morning glories covered the grey fence, and at dawn, the grey dreariness disappeared as morning glories bloomed. In the winter, piercing cold winds devastated flowers, but made it possible to play volleyball over the fence. Dark and light; bitter and sweet. Amid the darkness, joy comes in the morning.

Life is bittersweet. Just like the cross. Through Jesus, we can confess our sins and grieve the sins of others. Sin is the grey, the bitter. Jesus is the riot of color, the sweet.

Memories are riddled with complexity. Some are positive, some negative, some a combination of both. One of my earliest pre-verbal memories is feeling warm when the radiator came on in the apartment. The heat was turned off at night, and each morning when the janitor put coal in the furnace the air lost its nasty chill. At 10:00 p.m. the temperature would slowly but steadily decrease; at 6:00 a.m. it would slowly rise.

I loved the bustle of the city and the excitement of holidays. I loved the warmth and peace of the church. I loved my friends, dolls, reading and learning new things. However, I dreaded cold, bleak winters, and the dark shadows infiltrating my life physically, mentally, socially, and spiritually. Challenged by the ups and downs, the joy, and pain, I lived one day at a time.

I did not understand what life had been like for my parents as children, both born of poor immigrant parents. Far from home, with little education or resources, these brave families made a bold move to forge a new path in a promising world. Though strong in faith, they faced extreme hardships and tragic losses.

My mother's grandfather died before her birth, and her father died suddenly of appendicitis when she was seven years old. My mother yearned for love after her father's premature death and married at 18 years of age. She conceived two children prior to her 24th birthday. My mother's marriage, like many others during World War II, dissolved due to distance and physical needs. She lived heart-broken, disillusioned and alone.

She met and married my father not long after. Both my grandfather and my father struggled with alcoholism, and both became aggressive when drinking. I heard stories of my grandfather's abuse and witnessed my father's violence myself. Both of my grandfathers died before I was born, so I had no experience being loved by a grandfather.

My grandmother died when I was seven years old. My mother, reeling from profound grief after her mother's death from cancer, stopped going to church. She distanced herself from relatives strong in faith, consumed by anger at God for allowing her mother to die.

Grief crippled her faith. "The good die young," she said. My parents separated soon after, and following three more years of violence, they divorced. My mother remarried, and a few months later we moved to a different state.

I continued to go to church, but after the move, I was not connected with a specific faith group. In high school, I joined Youth for Christ (YFC), then attended youth camps, which re-ignited my desire for missions. However, I had so little Bible knowledge and walked away after being given an erroneous perspective on faith. Over time, God slowly faded in my life. Much of the time, my thoughts and behaviors turned to people, places, and things more worldly. I let Him in now and then, but He lost preeminence in my life.

Like many children, I had no interest in family history. But over the years, I learned much about my ancestors and the long line of spiritual warriors, primarily on my mother's side of the family. The wait was worth it. I might not have appreciated the generations of faith if I had met my relatives during my young adulthood, as I was grieving unfulfilled promises and pursuing misguided desires and dreams.

I've since connected with some of the more distant relatives and delight in learning more about life in Sweden, the families, and their faith journeys. Records dating as far back as the 1500s indicate my ancestors were people of strong, gripping faith. They carried their faith to the new world and served as missionaries or planted churches. One ancestor (a woman) founded the first Swedish Evangelical Free Church in Texas. Another, a missionary statesman, served in foreign missions for more than fifty years. Colleagues affectionately call him "Uncle Jack." Another family owns a 1541 first edition of the *Gustav Vasa Bible*, which is permanently on loan to the local church for everyone to enjoy.

I learned what life was like in Sweden during the 1800s. It was mandatory to go to church, so longboats were constructed to carry villagers to the church. Most of my ancestors lived near water and immigrated by sea to America. The older I become, the more family and family history means to me. It helps me better understand aspects of myself, the call to missions, and my love for water.

I wondered how my family got off track spiritually. Even though they had a rich Christian heritage, my immediate and most of my extended family drifted away. I talked with my cousin "Uncle Jack" and asked, "What happened to my side of the family? How did we stray so far from the truth?"

Jack was silent. Then he said, "I think it was the men they married."

I took a breath, considering his answer. I understood. Choices. How life-altering destructive choices can be. I thought about the Scripture, 2 Timothy 3:6-7: "They are the kind who worm their way into homes and gain control over gullible women, who are loaded down with sins and are swayed by all kinds of desires, always learning but never able to come to a knowledge of the truth."

The fallen world and the choices made have lasting impact on not only those who live through them, but on those who come after. The children's children reap gains and losses from those who came before. My mother spent many years searching for relief from emotional and physical pain, until one day, she surrendered her heart, her hemiplegic body, and her self-sufficiency to Jesus. Desperate for healing, she listened to Oral Roberts' television broadcast each day, and I believe, found the relief she had so unsuccessfully sought for years. I wish my mother had shared her rekindled faith with me, but I can cherish memories of her peaceful transition from this life to the next. Sleeping in her hospital room, the Holy Spirit woke me just as she took her last breath. I didn't know it was Him, but His presence gave me peace as well.

Decades went by before my faith was rekindled. Desperation leads to change. Some people, including me, tolerate what we consider normal, even if it is painful. We stay on a destructive path because we have become comfortable with it and because we don't know what else to do. We appear solid, yet our core is fragmented. The façade may fool many, including ourselves.

At some point, destructive paths become deadly paths. This downward spiral from destructive to deadly breaks through deception and triggers an altered response. God is long-suffering. He waits, and He waits. He knows when and what circumstances will shake the blinders from our eyes. To break free, we must make different choices. I needed to make different choices.

I chose to return to Jesus, my first Love, in 1991. He is the One who loves me more than any human is capable of. My desperation to share what I received precipitated initial steps into missions. The vision was before me, but it required careful and consistent forward movement.

Chapter Three

Stark Realities

I joined a mission trip going to Hong Kong in 1993, enticed by my love for distant lands and people of other cultures. What solidified my decision was the objective of the project—smuggling Bibles into Hong Kong through a ministry called Donkeys for Jesus. I reflected on my childhood as I prepared for my first ever mission trip. I clearly look at the world through the lens of bittersweet. Foods, experiences, and life itself can be bittersweet. Sometimes bitter and sweet occur together. Other times we may crumble under bitter or bask and delight in sweet. Bittersweet memories of my childhood came to mind.

China was deep in my spirit after going to China Town in Chicago as a young child, where I entered a world different from my own. I savored the atmosphere: the colors, sights, sounds, tastes, and the energy. I knew this day was significant—might I travel one day? I often dreamed of far-away places. Countless people, bustling activity with never-ending opportunities to learn. The trip to China Town had a significant impact on me as it gave me a glimpse of life as I would come to know it years down the road.

On a typical day, I wandered through my neighborhood, visiting older adults who lived alone. I sat on their steps, captivated, as I listened to their stories and learned about different cultures. Chicago was a "melting pot," so I traveled the world as neighbors shared memories of years gone by. Immigrants from Belgium, Poland, Germany, Sweden, Italy, and Puerto Rico settled in my neighborhood, sharing snippets of life in distant parts of the world. Gang activity was frequent, with adolescents carrying chains and other weapons. They tended to ignore the children, so in general, I was unaffected by their struts down the alley. I lived in my world of babushkas, balls, fences, and Swedish and Polish delicacies.

Childhood dreams became reality. I was going to China as an ambassador of Jesus, carrying what I believe to be the most important physical possession any of us can have—a Bible. My financial resources were small, but my faith was growing. The flight was crowded, the air turbulent, and I felt the familiar symptoms of motion sickness. Up and down, back and forth we went, my motion sickness symptoms increasing by the minute. I prayed, "Jesus, heal me, please." Immediately, the symptoms subsided. The Holy Spirit said, "Believe, and you shall receive." I did not experience motion sickness again during the entire trip, even though we traveled over land, sea, and air. Jesus answered my prayer and increased my faith.

Team members wore layers of clothes to hide tiny Bibles. I wore a slip under my dress with pockets, and due to my small stature, the slip was too long for me. I found it difficult to climb into vehicles and walk up and down steps with Bibles bumping on my shins. Conflicting emotions stirred because carrying Bibles into mainland China was risky and a big step for me. I am typically an over-the-top rule-follower for fear of making mistakes or being rejected.

Our task was to carry and then later unload the Bibles in hidden spaces for members of the underground church to pick up. We hid them in bathroom stalls, closets, wherever we could find locations available to leave them. We never saw the people we served; this was sad for me as I love to be with people and partner in ministry with the nationals. However, the mission was accomplished. The passion of the Chinese Church stirred my faith, and the people strengthened my resolve to change the world for good.

The last day, the team visited Hong Kong harbor for a view of the city. On the way to the lookout, team members shopped for souvenirs. I mused how in the past I would have joined them and would have missed the opportunity to spend time alone with God and His creation. Not that it was wrong for people to buy souvenirs, but my destructive past required I cling to Jesus and not people or things. I climbed the steps with expectation.

The view at the top did not disappoint. I took a deep breath, immersed in the sights, sounds, and smells surrounding me. The scene was breathtaking, with tiny junks and fishermen. Houses of all shapes, sizes, colors and materials dotted the horizon. Boat whistles and rail car warnings floated gently to the pinnacle. High up, I could still smell fish and the harbor.

But something unexpected interrupted my peaceful moment. A voice in my head said, "I will give you the world if you bow down and serve me." I took a deep breath, recognizing that the thought was not my own, and it was not coming from the Holy Spirit.

Distinguishing voices takes time, but I've learned how to tell them apart. When God speaks, either through Scripture, something another person says to you, or that "still, small voice" in your head, there is no fear. Rather, you know something you didn't know before, gain clarity on direction, or learn how to respond to a situation or person. And the Holy Spirit may use any of your five senses to draw you near to attend to what He wants you to receive.

A biblical worldview recognizes that both light and dark exist. There are two forces at work. In western cultures, many people of faith focus only on God, Jesus, the Holy Spirit, or all three. In most areas of the world, to talk about or believe only in the goodness of God while denying darkness causes one to be viewed as irrelevant or lacking credibility. I've learned that by omitting or denying the existence of evil, people in many cultures will listen as you speak, but then discount what you say. They know evil exists. Some tragically emphasize the power of evil over the power of Light.

I considered the stark reality of an ever-present spiritual realm of darkness. They know us. They know our desires and weaknesses. They constantly seek whom they may devour, and one way to do this is to put thoughts into our head. I disregarded the voice, because I knew it was not the Good Shepherd. I need not respond. I was at peace, and thankful I belonged to Jesus and no other spirit. How critical that we know the voice of God. How critical that we trust Him to change us, gaining what no one can take from us–love and belonging, life-giving purpose, security in Him now and forevermore.

This life-changing mission trip would not be my last. I knew missions was my future, but I had no idea God's plan was much larger than mine. In the meantime, I needed to take small steps to solidify the journey.

Jeff and I went to Mexico on a medical mission trip the next year. I heard tragic stories and learned many of the patients were involved in spiritism. The atmosphere was spiritually dark, and nights were debilitating and tormenting. I fervently prayed and worshipped every night, but with each new day, the spiritual struggle increased.

This would have been a good time to share my struggles with others, but I didn't want to risk confessing my weakness. I presumed if I did, I might not be considered again in the future. This was a mistake for two reasons. First, a principle of faith is we exponentially multiply spiritual power by praying together. Second, many believers fail to entrust the future to the One who designs His God-guided purposes for us before we are born. He knows when the timing is right. He orchestrates events in our lives to move us where He wants us. The Israelites spent forty years in the wilderness traveling only 250 miles because God knew they were not yet strong enough to face the giants living in the land. God's timing is perfect; sometimes we push ahead of God instead of keeping pace with Him.

The final morning, I joined the team planning to go to "the dump" where people lived among garbage heaps. My world was shaken, however, when my interpreter was needed in the clinic, cancelling our trip to the dump. I was frustrated. I wanted to prove my faith was stronger than my fear, but God's mercy prevented me from going. The battle was bigger than my fledgling faith could handle. He fought the battle for me when my fear opened the door to demonic activity, then put a hedge of protection around me.

Prior to the Mexico trip, I thought I had grown enough to fight the enemy by myself. I was wrong. On some level, I doubted that God's power defeated Satan's. The Holy Spirit said to me, "You give the enemy too much power. If you're serious, you must grow. Trust Me." Believing God exists and trusting in Him are not the same thing. I needed to grow in both. I made slow but steady progress. Scripture says the mustard seed is the smallest of all seeds; but when planted, it becomes the largest garden plant. My mustard seed faith was still a tender shoot.

Perhaps God opened the door to join the team for multiple reasons. Yes, I would be a clown in Vacation Bible School. Yes, I would assess, recommend treatment and pray for people with psychosis in the medical clinic. But equally important, I needed to grow spiritually and be ever vigilant. Taking mountains and conquering giants requires total attention, commitment, and, above all, the sovereignty of God.

Chapter Four

If You Don't Stand Firm

I took one more short-term trip before leaving for full-time missions. Southeast Asia Prayer Center (SEAPC) arranged a trip to Beijing, China in the summer of 1996. This was my second trip to China, and though the mission differed somewhat from the first, I was more comfortable having been introduced to the culture and spiritual atmosphere three years earlier. The project included not only hand-carrying Bibles for the underground church but also to climb Buddhist high places, praying for the nation. I knew I was to go.

When I called the airlines to book the ticket, the only available return ticket was for three weeks, not two weeks. I'd made a promise to God that if I went on mission trips without Jeff, I would not be away longer than two weeks. Jeff had a mission trip planned to Dominica for two weeks, and I previously committed to a women's organization to speak the second Saturday. What would I do? The reservationist waited for my answer.

Suddenly, a Scripture from my prayer time that morning came to mind – "If you do not stand firm in your faith, you will not stand at all." (Isaiah 7:9b).

"Yes," I said. "I will book the ticket." This decision tested my faith, since it required that I leave Jeff in Washington D.C., unsure of when I would return.

The team flew to China and met with Mark Geppert, the founder of SEAPC. We carried Bibles to our hotel and stored them in the closet. The plan was compromised, which required we haul

Bible-filled duffel bags to a nearby restaurant to meet members of the underground church. The dinner was part of the original plan; but thirty people carrying a literal ton of Bibles in duffel bags was not. Remarkably, policemen did not pay any attention to thirty Americans dragging matching duffel bags down the street. These are the moments you are thankful to be invisible—present in body but unnoticed. May "the enemy" see Jesus or no one at all when we walk out kingdom business.

Dinner with leaders from the underground church made a significant impact on me. The local missionary gave us magnets showing how God's redemptive story is nestled in the Chinese language, and we heard remarkable stories from heroes of faith.

Mabel, a 93-year-old woman, still climbed mountains in Tibet sharing the gospel. Teacher Bi told us he was imprisoned for seventeen years for not denying that Jesus is Lord. He shared how he survived torture and persecution by cleaning the latrine. Since no one wanted this distasteful job, it gave him a secret place to praise God and quote Scriptures he held in his memory and heart. Overcoming the stench, shoveling human waste, he declared the first few verses of Psalm 27. "The Lord is my light and my salvation—whom shall I fear? The Lord is the stronghold of my life—of whom shall I be afraid?" Might I ever have that level of humility, courage, and trust in You, Lord?

The primary mission was for teams to climb the Buddhist high places, and Teacher Bi was the leader of my team. Mount Jiuhua, known as one of these four great holy sites in China, is situated in the southern portion of Anhui province. The mountain hosts ninety-nine peaks and covers an area of more than 100 kilometers. Considered the first mountain in Southeast China, its highest peak is 1,341 meters above sea level. Tianti sits here, the high place Temple. A Buddhist whose heart is set on pilgrimage must climb straight up for more than 1,000 steps to reach the top.

We took a night train from Beijing to Nanjing, a surreal experience. The clamor of the train, sleeping in a compartment with Chinese passengers, and noodles splashing with the movement of the cars created a vivid sensory experience. This was my first and only experience using a hole in the train floor as a latrine. I slept poorly, concerned I might miss my destination.

The next morning, we arrived in Nanjing, and the team stayed in housing near the base of the mountain. I faced another restless night. Most of my team members were young girls frightened by the spiritual atmosphere. We filled our backpacks for the day, prayed, and then began the climb. An early start increased probability we would reach the top to catch the last cable car of the day. I fasted throughout the climb.

Reaching the first level of the high place was pleasant and relatively easy. We saw beautiful statues of Kwan Yin, and other aesthetically pleasing gods. We heard what sounded like tinkling bells, but soon realized it was a chorus of singing birds. Melodious music nearly lulled sojourners to sleep. The climb became more difficult – and it was raining. The stones were uneven. Some were deep and others narrow; some were long but others short; many slanted in different directions. All of them, wet with rain and slippery, led us slowly and painstakingly upward toward the top.

The second level was dramatically different, an ominous and oppressive atmosphere. No feminine statues or dainty singing birds to break the silence. The temple was dark, damp and cold, with glass cases on the wall depicting people being tortured. The "king" in these temple cases demanded much. He tortured the people when less than expected was given, or gifts were inadequate.

Monks, with eyes glazed over, beat their drums as if in a trance. They seemed unaware that people wandered about, and the spirit of fear was present and intense. Fear resisted, even though we prayed with our minds and with our prayer languages. We started worshipping Jesus instead of battling in prayer. As we worshipped, demonic spirits fled, and the presence of God filled the temple. Our worship ushered in His sweet yet powerful presence. The monks did not understand English, giving us the opportunity to say, "God bless you." We asked Jesus to bring them His gift of salvation.

We continued upward, but half of our group of twelve decided they could pray from the hotel instead of climbing the high place. I climbed along with five others. The journey was arduous, and rain became storms. The terrain flooded, and the stones grew increasingly slippery. At one point, I needed to cross a suspension bridge over raging waters. I hesitated momentarily, captured by my former taskmaster, fear. *Help me, Father*, I prayed. He answered by having me recall a favorite poem:

I came to the swift, raging river;
the sound held the echo of fear.
I said, "Give me grace to fly over,
if you are as you promised quite near."
But He said, "Trust the grace I am giving,
all pervasive, sufficient for you;
take my hand we will face this together,
but My plan is not over, but through."[2]

I took a deep breath, then gingerly crept across the bridge. I was not alone. God held my hand.

Exhaustion overtook me from the long climb. At forty-five years old, I clearly found the climb more demanding than the teenage girls on the team. My clothes were soaked, my tired muscles strained. I was never an accomplished climber, though I love to walk and relish spectacular views at the summit. The other five team members were out of sight, and probably already on the way down. I stood motionless, since I could not advance but also would not retreat.

Two young Chinese men moved ahead of me, which interrupted my momentary paralysis. They talked with me, curious about an American climbing the high place. It would be disrespectful to stand still when these men were having a conversation with me. They climbed out of sight, but at my weakest point, God used them to increase my level of physical and spiritual endurance. By late afternoon, the two men were on their way down. They smiled as they passed me and said, "The turtle wins the race." Dedication, patience, perseverance, and faith. I must make it to the high place.

I reached the pinnacle several hours later, my body spent but my spirit soaring. I mastered the physical climb, but as I entered the cold, stone high place, my soul withered. Is this it? No birds, no drums, no monks, no signs of celebration? The high place was eerily void except for lifeless stone masks protruding from the ceiling. Rather than pomp and circumstance, I found emptiness. I closed my eyes and sighed with disappointment. I planned to spend hours in prayer, but darkness had settled in during my slow climb. I needed to take the cable car down before they stopped running. *Father, is this all there is? Did we accomplish anything by coming here?* The Holy Spirit answered, "Six people, bought by the blood of Jesus, praying all the way. The victory was in the climb."

I pondered my journey, descending the mountain by cable car. The Holy Spirit compared this high place with a life of sin. Sin is pleasant when we enter. It stimulates one or more of our senses, and we feel the rush of adrenalin and sensual pleasure. But continuing the path of sin becomes a stronghold, leading to fear, torment, and a host of other problems. Eventually, just as in my climb, we reach a stone fortress. This fortress is death—physical, mental, social, and spiritual. Like the climb, the journey begins with light, but ever so slowly, darkness slithers in and saturates every fiber of our being. There is no need for torment once the high place is reached. You are no longer alive. You are empty and alone. For some, this is eternal death.

> Journal entry, July 14, 1996
>
> Here we are in Jiuhua. I am struck by the natural beauty on the one hand, and the depth of oppression of the people on the other. People in Beijing hustling and bustling as in any big city with only a temporal purpose, and those in Jiuhua mesmerized by the incantations and incense. The steady beating of the drums and the bells—the looks of total confusion or torment on their faces. This is a web of religious confusion. Variations of Buddhism, Taoism, among others, converging in one spiritual center.

> Watching the people suffer their way to the temples, bowing every one to three steps grieves me as I see the burden they carry. Isaiah 26 declares that the former taskmasters are dead and will rise no more. Oh, to share the love of Jesus. But perhaps it is better His love shows through our smiles and touch and songs. Perhaps it is by our inability to speak the same language we have been able to praise and pray. Only God knows.
>
> Whatever we've done to share His Spirit—have we effectively punched holes in the spiritual cloud covering that suffocates the inhabitants of this beautiful valley nestled among the mountains? This mountain shall be removed. His glory shall go forth among the nations. Breathe life into these dry bones, oh God, with life everlasting. These bones can live.

The teams returned to Beijing after climbing three different Buddhist high places, and I stood on the promise that someone would exchange tickets with me. In those days, people exchanged tickets often, but no one offered. For two weeks, I waited for an answer to my prayer, and confessed I trusted God would get me home in time to pick up Jeff. I quoted Hebrews 11:6, "And without faith it is impossible to please God, because anyone who comes to him must believe that He exists and that He rewards those who earnestly seek him." I was sure the Holy Spirit led me to purchase the ticket.

The day before I hoped to leave, a young man said he would love to exchange tickets so he could stay longer. Thank God, I thought. My Father did not disappoint; I heard Him correctly when I purchased the tickets. He gave me the opportunity to grow in faith by purchasing a ticket for the wrong date and not providing an answer until the day before I left. Learning to hear the voice of God is a lifelong journey. My faith becomes stronger when I walk by faith, rather than by sight.

Several of us were to leave the next day, so we had a significant time of prayer. One of the young women said she heard the Holy Spirit say some people were to leave their Bibles for the underground Church, and that each of us should pray about it. I prayed—but I knew the Holy Spirit would not ask for mine since it was my lifeline and a leather-bound Bible from a man of faith I deeply respected.

I heard a still, small voice: "Give them your Bible." *What? No, Lord, please, not my Bible.* I hesitated, but I also knew obedience and sacrificial giving please God. I begrudgingly brought it to Mark and said, "I believe I'm supposed to leave my Bible. But they don't know English. Will anyone be able to use it?"

Mark said, "Yes, I know just the man. He knows English."

I said, "But will he cry when he gets it?"

Mark said, "Yes, he will cry."

So, I handed over my most precious possession. When I asked the girl who heard the word to leave our Bibles if she left hers, she said, "Oh, I didn't leave mine. The Holy Spirit didn't tell me to."

The entire experience made absolutely no sense to me, but as I considered it, my Bible had become an idol. It had more importance to me than Jesus. Jesus IS the Word. Nothing is more important than Him. My dependency needs to be on Jesus, not on the Bible itself. All things serve Him.

The next day, I started the journey back to the US to pick up Jeff and speak at the women's conference. Afterward, the group leaders wrote, "It is those who live on the edge who see the greatest miracles of our Lord. Your trust in the Lord encourages us to step out further."

Daring to Live on the Edge. This was my new reality. The China missions, among others, increased my faith and inspired me to step out when I could not see the ground under me. They encouraged me to live on the edge, come what may. I began to walk the destiny God created for my life.

Chapter Five

On the Road

My sister gave me a water bottle which reads, "You can never cross the ocean unless you have the courage to lose sight of the shore." Short-term missions stirred my faith for greater things. Leaving Ordinary, Virginia, would open wide the door to sail through natural and spiritual seas.

The time had come to step out in faith. I mailed my application to Mercy Ships, and though I had not received a response, I gave notice at the church and at the counseling practice. I knew Jeff and I could not join a ship since single parents were not accepted on board, so I planned to work at the International Office until he started college. I hoped to serve on board one day.

Soon after, I received a call from Mercy Ships with news of acceptance to the Discipleship Training School (DTS). I thought, *I need to pray.* I didn't need to pray about whether I wanted to go. I needed to pray about whether I would succeed. I went to the empty sanctuary and knelt at the altar. *Oh God, am I ready for this? I have failed so many times. Can I leave LightHouse and survive? Will I keep my mind? Can I keep my faith? Can I keep my son?*

"Yes," He said. "The anchor holds." His soft answer did not disappoint.

Jeff and I prepared for transition. A friend and I sold most of our belongings and believed it was at the Holy Spirit's leading. We both knew it was a critical step in our faith journey. Many thought we had lost our minds as we set up a garage sale in the church parking lot. People grabbed items with such speed we nearly lost family pictures and other special memories. Determined to be free for all God had for us, we sold item after item, encumbrance after encumbrance.

My mind flooded with memories of my journey, and God's presence in it. For years, I dreaded getting out of bed without a light on during the night. Things had changed. As I walked back to my room without lights one night, the Holy Spirit said, "You used to need the light. Now you are the light." Jesus shines His light through human vessels. He turned my darkness into light.

The Scripture the Holy Spirit gave me as I prepared for missions was Matthew 9:35-38:

> Jesus went through all the towns and villages, teaching in their synagogues, proclaiming the good news of the kingdom and healing every disease and sickness. When he saw the crowds, he had compassion on them, because they were harassed and helpless, like sheep without a shepherd. Then he said to his disciples, "The harvest is plentiful, but the workers are few. Ask the Lord of the harvest, therefore, to send out workers into his harvest field." (Matthew 9:35-38)

A few days later, Jeff and I packed our remaining belongings for the journey ahead. When I told the friends who had given us the car that we were heading to Texas, they looked terror-stricken. They had never intended for the car to go beyond the local area and feared we would be stranded. Another friend said, "An anchor is used to keep you in place; to keep you from drifting off. I think you can go on trips, but you are to stay here, held by the anchor."

Unsettled but determined, I said, "I'm leaving tomorrow with Jeff. I may be back, but I'm going." I was not running away; I was running toward. Jeff stood by me all the way.

Jeff and I safely reached our first destination after the car overheated. We stayed with another single mom and her two daughters in North Carolina for one month, waiting for the next DTS to begin at Mercy Ships. A Christian school generously allowed Jeff to attend at no charge, so we settled in for a brief stay while making plans.

I knew I was destined for Mercy Ships. The battered car barely ran, but I hoped it would somehow make the trip to Texas and serve as our transportation during the five months of training. A close friend, however, offered to give me a slightly newer, more reliable car if I could drive the old one from North Carolina to Florida to make the exchange.

"Yes," I said. "Thank you so very much."

God had provided again.

I expected the drive to Florida to be long, but uncomplicated. However, the day I departed, a hurricane loomed ahead. *Should I go, or should I forego?* I wondered. The DTS was starting soon, and this was my last opportunity. I decided to brave the storm and drive overnight to Florida. Jeff stayed with my friends, and they sent me off with prayer and much misgiving. "Let us know when you arrive," the mom said.

Rain poured and winds challenged my tiny, but God-propelled car. Trees cluttered the road, and the sky grew darker by the minute. *It's a long way to Florida,* I thought. *Help me, Father. Keep me awake, please.* I remembered the drive when the car overheated, how I often drive in the dark, but that God is ever in the midst. I arrived in Florida—exhausted but astonished by the undeniable love and faithfulness of God. The return trip to North Carolina was seamless, and each day was one step closer to dream fulfillment.

Jeff and I attended a small church with our friends during the short stay in North Carolina. Jeff had no idea what thoughts plagued my mind. Obstacles we faced along the way shook my resolve. During one service, the pastor interrupted his message on two occasions to confirm God had a plan for Jeff's life. We didn't know the pastor, so this increased our faith the word was from God. But I thought, *What about me, Lord? I'm the one responsible for the move to Texas, and the potential pitfalls. Please speak to me, too.*

We went forward for communion and the pastor said to me, "How have you found such favor with God He entrusted this son to you?" Yet again, peace settled in because the Holy Spirit spoke directly to my doubts. God heard my prayers, traveled with us, and revealed His plans.

Psalm 37:3-4 reads, "Trust in the Lord and do good; dwell in the land and enjoy safe pasture. Take delight in the Lord, and he will give you the desires of your heart." Jesus gave me the desires of my heart, because I chose to trust Him, to follow Scripture, and to serve others; perhaps most of all because I stepped out in faith.

Remarkable similarities exist between my sojourn to Texas and the emigration of my Scandinavian ancestors to America in the mid-to-late 1800s. In some cases, the husband traveled before the wife and children. Their strength and determination, along with their courage and sense of adventure, inspire me—especially the women traveling across the Atlantic Ocean with babies in tow. They modeled how to navigate uncertainty, upheaval, and potential disappointment. Just like my ancestors, Jeff and I left for Texas to live the dream, come what may.

God told Abraham to leave his home, though Abraham did not know where God planned to take him. God later led the Israelites out of bondage in Egypt to the Promised Land and provided a pillar of fire by night and a cloud by day to lead them. I nearly panicked as I drove along dark roads but encouraged myself with my faith. I knew His voice. I knew the difference between natural and supernatural voices around me. With no end in sight, I trusted God's compass. Just as He led Abraham and the Israelites, He led me. I prayed my little light would shine, grow brighter and brighter, clearer and clearer until the full light of day.

Leaving Ordinary, Virginia, I was unaware that my life would pivot in a second town, Uncertain, Texas. But for now, we were on our way to Mercy Ships. God miraculously and providentially watched over us along the way.

Chapter Six

Unwanted Reflection

Jeff and I arrived in Texas mid-September 1996. We both wondered what this new season offered, but we trusted God led us there. The vision of Mercy Ships, a faith-based global charity founded in 1978, is to follow the 2,000-year-old model of Jesus, providing hope and healing to the world's poor. With 15 national offices and over 450 crew from more than 40 countries serving on board, Mercy Ships' impact is huge.

Mercy Ships uses hospital ships to fulfill its vision, and there have been multiple ships over several decades. The flagship, the *Anastasis*, an Italian passenger vessel, housed 350 crew members after refitting as a hospital ship. Other smaller ships, including the *Good Samaritan*, the *Pacific Ruby*, and the *Island Mercy*, served in various locations with fewer crew members. The *Caribbean Mercy*, a Norwegian cargo ship, served for twelve years after refit with an in-port crew of 150. Over time, these ships were phased out of service, yet each one made a significant impact in the nations where they traveled.

Mercy Ships currently has two functioning ships, the *Africa Mercy* and the *Global Mercy*. The *Africa Mercy* was a Danish rail ferry before it was refit as a hospital ship and carries up to 450 crew members. The latest ship, the *Global Mercy*, is the first ship built from the ground up as a hospital ship, carrying a crew of 450 as well. The *Global Mercy* is large enough to fit all the previous ships inside its massive structure. An additional ship will soon be under construction.

But Mercy Ships is more than a fleet of ships. Without the people who serve onboard, through off-ship programs and in support services at national offices, the ships would only be impressive hunks of metal. Just like Jesus, Mercy Ships crew and staff have tender hearts for suffering people.

Environmental conditions like poverty and war have a devastating impact on the whole person—body, soul, spirit, and relationships. In addition to world-class, life-changing surgeries, Mercy Ships programs seek to bring healing to those neglected or abandoned for conditions that might be considered frightening or repulsive to some people. Facial tumors, other deformities, inability to control urine or stool, mental/emotional trauma, among others, lead to isolation and despair. These conditions are typically seen as the result of witchcraft in low-and-middle-income countries. Mercy Ships offers people with little or no hope physical, emotional, social, and spiritual care, demonstrating the nature and character of a loving God.

The first step in joining Mercy Ships long-term required participation in a Discipleship Training School (DTS). When I joined in 1996, Mercy Ships was part of the Youth With A Mission (YWAM) family of ministries, and DTS was an integral part of both organizations. DTS included three months of lecture and two months of field service to share common perspectives on faith, and to gain first-hand experience in the nations that are underserved.

I started the training with Mercy Ships, while Jeff attended high school nearby. I was secure in my professional educational development, and I was confident spiritual growth was what I needed most. I expected to grow in faith, but I was unprepared for the spiritual heart surgery I needed to endure to move forward in missions. Participants shared their life stories with such transparency; I was obligated to do the same.

My bittersweet journey—a blending of darkness and light, cold and warmth was both wonderful and terrible. Experiences are life-giving or destructive. Experiences, along with personality and perspective on faith, shape and influence how we navigate life.

I broached my childhood experiences with hesitation, and as I shared my story, pain, shame, and fear resurfaced. While shame and fear are different, they both constrict and cripple a sense of self-worth and healthy relationships with others. The curious, adventurous, energetic, and social person I was created to be took years to re-emerge after trauma.

My mother had met my practical needs but was generally distant and preoccupied. My father was violent when intoxicated and often absent. Both parents were married previously, and family life was predictably dysfunctional. My father had been out of the home since I was eight years old, and though he made multiple promises to visit me, he rarely arrived due to side trips to the local tavern. I only saw my father one time after we moved to a different state. I longed for him.

Treatment of girls and women was very different in the 50s and 60s. I was told I didn't need to go to college, since I should get married and have a family. Sayings I heard over and over were "Don't tell tales out of school," and "What happens in this house stays in this house." I grew up in this era and I had secrets.

I was sexually assaulted by both my father and my stepfather, and in addition, had several incidents of uninvited sexual advances as a young child and teenager. Inappropriate behaviors from the men in my life created intense confusion. My need to be loved, cherished, and held was overpowering. This, coupled with living in dysfunctional homes, contributed to the development of my own destructive lifestyle. The consequence was multiple marriages, abortion, years of medication, and hospitalizations for severe depression and post-traumatic stress disorder. Sharing my life with strangers and reliving unresolved traumatic experiences led to condemnation and night terror. It took weeks to face the pain I thought I had already processed.

For decades, I waited for my father to come back for me, but he never did. Many young girls long for a knight in shining armor—someone gallant, wise, invincible, and loving. Ultimately, I learned my Heavenly Father never left me, and He never will. I needed to reach out to Him because the perfect One waited for my return. His arms are powerful, safe, and everlasting.

Over the years, God put various lifesavers in my path for this very purpose. A friend wrote this Scripture in the front of my Bible during high school: "But seek first his kingdom and his righteousness, and all these things will be given to you as well." (Matthew 6:33). Each time I ignored the lifesavers, whether subtle or obvious, I moved further from who God created me to be.

Scripture addresses people who flounder, oblivious to the ever-present God who is keenly interested in being THE lifesaver. One significant Scripture is found in the Psalms:

> The Lord is gracious and compassionate, slow to anger and rich in love. The Lord is good to all; he has compassion on all he has made ... The Lord upholds all who fall and lifts up all who are bowed down. The eyes of all look to you, and you give them their food at the proper time. You open your hand and satisfy the desires of every living thing. (Psalm 145:8-9; 14-16)

Some of us never cry out for help or for rescue. Many people think God only rescues those who do the right thing, or those who know Him. They think we must be "good enough." In truth, none of us is "good enough." He has compassion on all He has made. All of us are imperfect and every one of us sins. That's why we all need a Savior who can pull us from the slimy pit when we plunge into sin or despair.

The Father's incredible love is expressed beautifully in Hosea:

> When Israel was a child, I loved him, and out of Egypt I called my son. But the more they were called, the more they went away from me. They sacrificed to the Baals and they burned incense to images. It was I who taught Ephraim to walk, taking them by the arms; but they did not realize it was I who healed them. I led them with cords of human kindness, with ties of love. To them I was like one who lifts a little child to the cheek, and I bent down to feed them. (Hosea 11:1-4)

Even before we ask, God soothes us and prepares our hearts to receive Him. He hates to see us wander. He weeps when we suffer. He heals and cares for us even when we don't appreciate it—even when we don't know that He exists, who He is, and that He heals. He ties us with cords of human kindness and bends down to feed us. He is a good Father. No father, not even the most excellent human father, can compare to Father God whose love in unfathomable.

The journey into my heart destabilized me. To intimately know God, I needed to leave many things at the foot of the cross. Wounds go deep, and we spend our natural lives trusting God to complete the good work—the healing—He so ably begins in us.

Insecurities clouded my perspective and wreaked havoc in my mind. I had decades of education and experience in the fields of psychiatry and psychology, contradicted by how I lived my life. I doubted I could ever serve others with my previous poor choices and residue following trauma. But one compassionate and wise DTS speaker said though I was not ready at the time, God would be faithful to see His plans fulfilled. I declared my past would not define or hinder me, yet realistically recognized I still needed to grow. I learned much about the Father Heart of God, and additional knowledge to facilitate healing for desperate people.

I met the international chaplain, (the person whose name Don had written on his boarding pass), and his wife mid-way during the training school. We had connected by phone a few months earlier, and the chaplain said if God called me, He would make room for my talents and gifts. I knew one day we would work together. Soon, our group of DTS participants and family members left for field service.

Seven weeks passed quickly. But something changed. Before DTS, I experienced God through my senses. I could hear His voice, see Him in visions and in creation, and feel His presence. Whether walking in the woods, laying on the beach, searching for exotic animals or sitting with domestic ones, I came closer to my Heavenly Father. I depended on sensorial input for comfort and direction. During DTS, the Holy Spirit spoke to me about ministry, but He was silent about anything personal—especially about Jeff and me.

Just before we returned to Mercy Ships from DTS field service, I heard God's still, small, inaudible voice. He did not abandon me; He was not angry or rejecting me. Rather, He pushed me out of the nest like a mother bird for my faith to grow. I needed to learn to trust Him, even when He did not speak—to know His character, His Word, His love. No matter the circumstances, He was present and listened. He had not, and would not, ever, leave or forsake me. He would never leave or forsake Jeff. We were His.

Chapter Seven

Sink or Swim

Missionary training was over, and I needed to make a choice. Would I return to Virginia or remain in Texas? People primarily leave the mission field because of inadequate finances or relational conflicts, and each of those reasons is complex and individual. Conflicts may occur among family members in transition or already be present before serving. There may be work-related conflicts existing among coworkers, leaders, or those being served in the nations. And people may either not have enough funds to cover usual expenses or have mission expenses which require additional support.

I came to Mercy Ships daring to live on the edge. I hadn't attended a specific church over the course of my entire life, so I lacked a support base to cover the cost of long-term missions. A friend suggested I apply for positions at a local hospital near Mercy Ships and wait to decide. I was offered a job in Human Resources, which was a perfect opportunity to use my doctorate by working with systems and individuals. Local work would cover expenses and would give me the opportunity to slowly increase my support base.

The decision was clear from a financial perspective, but I was conflicted about leaving my friends and mentors in Virginia. Jeff would be affected by the decision as well. I've learned over decades of transition that when you leave, life goes on as usual for the people left behind. Those who relocate carry the burden of responsibility to not only build new relationships but be proactive to maintain the ones they already have. It can be extremely lonely, especially when facing natural or spiritual battles. Ultimately, the desire to fulfill my God-given purpose was more important than the dread of lonely nights.

I took three trips with YWAM prior to full-time service with Mercy Ships. The first was to Greece to offer counseling for people who served in spiritually intense regions. Missionaries from several countries came together for equipping and rest. I understood the responsibilities, but did not expect an identity crisis. During one of the workshop sessions, the presenter asked the question, "Are you willing to sacrifice your mind for Christ?"

People who serve in missions expect to face physical, emotional, social, and spiritual challenges—perhaps even lose their lives. But God threw me a curve ball. I thought I was at the conference to support others, but I received a startling challenge. *Was I willing to sacrifice my mind? Would I do it for the sake of the gospel?*

The question unsettled me as I considered what that would mean. Loss of relationship; loss of independence; loss of productivity; loss of self. After a time of intense prayer, I said, *Yes, Father, I surrender all. Even my mind.*

The second was a trip to Bosnia in 1997. The government of the Yugoslav republic of Bosnia-Herzegovina declared independence in 1992. Bosnian Serb forces, combined with the Serb-dominated Yugoslav army, attacked and surrounded Sarajevo and other areas where Bosniaks (Bosnian Muslims) lived. Religious and ethnic differences triggered the conflict. Bosniaks are predominantly Muslim, Serbs are predominantly Orthodox Christians, and Croats are predominantly Catholic. Countless Bosniaks were driven into concentration camps. Women and girls were sexually assaulted by multiple people, and other civilians were tortured, starved and murdered. Reports indicate 100,000 people died, 80 percent of them Bosniak. The war ended in 1995, but the conflict and the arbitrary division of land left the country and its inhabitants devastated.

My responsibility was to provide training for local non-governmental organization (NGO) workers. I was not quite sure how to do this, since my focus in counseling integrated prayer and Scripture. The workers were Bosniak, and therefore Muslim. Then I remembered Maslow's Hierarchy of Needs, and that basic needs are universal. I developed a training seminar with Maslow as the model. Maslow's theory states there are five levels of basic needs necessary for individuals to achieve satisfaction: 1) Physiological needs; 2) safety and security; 3) love and belonging; 4) self-esteem; and 5) self-actualization. For faith-based purposes, I have adapted this model by changing self-actualization to a God-given purpose and have encircled the model with God since He meets every need.

I offered a workshop for a group of women, both resilient and determined to rebuild their community. After the workshop, the participants sent a spokesperson with a critical question. She said, "We understand these needs and how to meet them. But how do you get this?" She pointed to the second level, safety and security.

I said, "Are you asking me how I get those needs met?" She shook her head yes. I said, "I pray."

Her eyes lit up, and she ran to the group saying, "She prays." The women all smiled and nodded in agreement. No one is invincible. No one is promised tomorrow. Through my own terrifying journey, I learned the only security is in Jesus, who promises me eternity with Him. These women received strength and hope by seeking God as they faced death and destruction.

A quiet Muslim woman is forever etched in my mind. Her face was ragged yet hopeful and, though hunched over, she carried herself in a dignified way. I learned she had eleven children, and her husband and some of her children had disappeared. She was relocated to two different countries before she returned to her devastated homeland. We exchanged few words, but I was impressed to give her something—anything. I had a bottle of costly perfume a friend bought for me. I gave it to the woman and said, "You are precious to God."

She looked deeply into my eyes, and said, "Everyone is precious to God."

I witnessed true beauty rising from ashes.

Our team joined a group of Bosniaks determined to rebuild their village. They planned workdays with large groups of people to face the seemingly insurmountable needs. We found mounds of rubble around every corner, and houses were damaged or demolished. Clearing debris would take months—perhaps years. The work was grueling; the ground was uneven and dangerous, and the dust from broken buildings made it difficult to breathe.

I had trouble breathing for another reason. I looked up and saw a jeep packed with Serbian soldiers driving through the village. Though they did not speak, the hate in their eyes, their defiance, and demonstration of power unnerved me. Serbian soldiers drove by to intimidate, even though they no longer had ownership of the land. I learned first-hand that Bosniaks came in large groups for more than the overwhelming task. Numbers provide safety. It reminded me of the Scripture where Nehemiah told the workers to carry a weapon in one hand and a tool for work in the other. I marveled at the tenacity of the men, women, and children, choosing to move forward when it would be easier to turn back.

I saw destruction everywhere as I traveled through the countryside. Survivors joined together to search for loved ones in mass graves. The buildings were riddled with bullets, and the terrain violated with buried land mines. Some intentionally discovered; others by accidentally stepping or driving on one. Tape barricades marked identified land mines. I noticed one area taped off, and a dog walking toward it. I thought, *What if the dog goes inside? What if it was an infant or a young child?* Bosniaks lived with this fear every day.

I developed a subconscious prejudice toward Serbians through these experiences, but God in His wisdom gave me the opportunity the next year to work in Croatia with seven Serbian believers. I was guarded because I had hardened my heart toward them the year before. A team member, an interpreter and I attended an intimate service with three Serbian priests in a carved-out enclave storefront. I melted when one of the priests said "Lord, have mercy on us" in English. Their humility and love for God broke through my prejudice. We all have prejudices. We just don't know we have them.

May God show us how we can love our neighbors as ourselves. The trip to Bosnia enlarged my worldview.

A year later, I knew it was time to apply for a position in Mercy Ships, so I contacted the director of human resources, and he said there was an opening in HR. We met at, of all places, a fast-food chicken restaurant. His smile was contagious, and he seemed bewildered anyone chose to work in HR. The director was delighted I had asked to join, and I was thrilled my time had come. I formally joined the HR department of Mercy Ships in 1998, and the team provided a welcoming and safe place to begin my long-term journey into missions.

Unlike many mission organizations, Mercy Ships accepts single parents and gives them flexible hours to be home with their children when they return from school. Single parents must work somewhere—why not serving God in missions? It was not possible to serve long term on a ship as a single parent, but there was an open door at the international office.

The core values of Mercy Ships are to love God, love and serve others, be people of integrity, and strive for excellence in all we say and do. I thought, *I have found where I belong*. Signing the Religious Order Covenant was a privilege. After a destructive life serving myself, God moved me toward a life of selflessness. Covenanting to live by Godly principles encouraged and humbled me. It was a sacred act.

An earthquake and mudslides ravaged Nicaragua soon after I joined. The *Caribbean Mercy* had left Nicaragua just weeks before, but purposed a return visit to provide post crisis care for those who remained. I provided counseling in a remote village where we set up a medical clinic and met with many patients suffering from fear and anxiety due to trauma. Patients lined up for counseling and prayer while I sat under a tree. During a time of incredible loss, those who stood in line were hopeful. And the team members gave tirelessly of themselves to provide medical care to whosoever would come. I caught a glimpse of my future.

With heavy hearts, we walked across the mudslides where nearly 2,000 people, including entire villages, lay buried under the mud. Dead animals and ravaged trees were grave reminders of the loss. Then I noticed a tiny branch with a few budding leaves. Yes. New life emerges. There is always hope. God relentlessly redeems not only land, but people.

In 2000, I combined a work trip with a graduation present for Jeff, and we joined the *Anastasis* in the Canary Islands. After sailing to London, we visited the *Africa Mercy*, a rail ferry being refitted as a hospital ship. We attended a service on board, where the DTS speaker said to Jeff, "You are called to do something you really do not want to do; but the Holy Spirit will not let you go." This confirmed that Jeff's call to theater and film was God's choice and not his own. The speaker said to me, "You will train leaders internationally, and your words will be apples of gold in settings of silver." Those prophetic words strengthened us as we overcame challenges, both physical and spiritual.

In the fall of 2000, I traveled to Free Town, Sierra Leone, to provide HR support to a land-based medical team called New Steps. Over 15,000 people with polio lived in the area, and the ministry made a huge impact. The trip to Sierra Leone was significant for many reasons, but most importantly, I learned I was not designed to live long term in low-and-middle-income countries. I was called to make shorter trips, just as my friend said before I left for Mercy Ships. I'm anchored in the United States, but my anchor has a very large chain. It holds me no matter where I go, and my anchor is Jesus.

A few months later, I was offered a split position between Chaplaincy and Health Care Services (HCS). As a chaplain, I assisted with meetings, provided counseling, and occasionally accompanied crew members in crisis back to their homes. In HCS, I developed policies and procedures. A year later, I moved into a full-time chaplaincy position, which gave opportunities to serve short-term on both the *Caribbean Mercy* and the *Africa Mercy*, in addition to my regular responsibilities at the International Support Center. Daily onboard experiences such as watching welders transforming the *Africa Mercy* into a hospital ship brought me to tears; shadowing medical teams on board the *Caribbean Mercy* in the Dominican Republic stirred my passion.

Over time, Mercy Ships became not only my ministry but part of my family. Early on, I guarded my heart because I formed attachments and then people left. Some people come for a short time; others stay for decades. It's painful to watch those you love leave. But as the years passed, I also saw many return, and old friendships were rekindled. Mercy Ships is a vibrant, dynamic, and life-giving organism of which I was grateful to belong.

I sat for the oral portion of the psychologist licensing exam for a third time while in Chaplaincy. I did not need the psychologist license to practice, since I had decades of experience as an advanced practice psychiatric clinical nurse specialist. Industrial and organizational psychologists rarely seek licensure, as it is unnecessary as a consultant to organizations; however, being a licensed psychologist increased my credibility and scope. The exam process requires two reviewers to reach an agreement on pass or fail, so after taking the exam, those being examined sit in a room waiting to learn if a decision has been reached. If there isn't agreement, a second oral exam happens the same day. If the reviewers agree on pass or fail, the examinee is sent home and receives results six weeks later. Twice before I sat for the exam; both times I failed. All three times I took the exam, I was the last person in the room called to take the exam, and the last person to leave the room following the examiners' decision.

The first time, something significant happened while I waited to take the exam. Sitting in the large, intimidating room, my eyes were drawn to a *Time* magazine with the cover title: "Africa Rising." As I read the article, it shared the story of a child soldier named Felfiel, who became a killing machine in the Mozambique conflict; how through witchcraft his trauma was healed, and he was received back into the community. The article stated, "The community tradition worked better than any modern forms of psychotherapy."[3]

I was intrigued by the article, yet perplexed by the assertion that witchcraft was more effective than psychotherapy. I wondered how this would play out in my life. I took the oral exam, then waited the agonizing six weeks. The results indicated I failed due to "crippling anxiety."

The second time I failed again. Though I had been an extrovert as a child, life experience "crippled" my confidence and sense of adequacy. Written exams were easy; I passed the written for both nursing and psychology on the first attempt. Yet again, for the second time, I sat before two male interviewers, with a one-way mirror hiding a videographer and licensing evaluators. I just could not process the content.

When I sat for the exam a third time, my goals had changed. I no longer focused on the outcome. If I failed, I would not take it again. I didn't need the license as an industrial and organizational psychologist. This time I had two goals: 1) I would say exactly what

I thought; and 2) I would not be intimidated. A friend sent me off with cards to read every hour to calm my nerves and focus on Jesus.

Yet again, two men interviewed me. One of them reviewed for the first time, as evidenced by his dry mouth. I thought, *I have been through this before, and I am calmer than the reviewer.* The topic was international health care and cultural issues, which was my specialty. I knew some of my answers were not what they wanted to hear—but I stood firm. Six weeks later, I learned I passed. The personal victory was standing up to human and spiritual intimidation.

It's easy to slip into complacency and think we have arrived. When I left for Mercy Ships, I thought the road going forward would be much more comfortable, but I was wrong. Walking through the oral exam process was painful, but at the same time required I grow to succeed. The exam itself was irrelevant. What was critical for advancing my kingdom purpose was personal growth in confidence and courage, and the pace of my progress depended on my willingness to surrender comfort to become more like Jesus. Life reminds us how far we have come, but we are still on the journey.

In Luke 7:22, Jesus sends John's disciples back to John the Baptist to share this message, "Go back and report to John what you have seen and heard: The blind receive sight, the lame walk, those who have leprosy are cleansed, the deaf hear, the dead are raised, and the good news is proclaimed to the poor." I became part of an organization whose mission was to follow Jesus through acts of service to bring hope and healing. With the privilege, comes responsibility—I don't represent myself alone; I represent a global organization. Will I represent it well?

I stepped on to an international stage. I no longer faced only my own trauma. I was now entrusted with the responsibility of assisting others in the painful process. My personal survivor skills were insufficient for the deluge. Luke 22:31-32 says, "Simon, Simon, Satan has asked to sift all of you as wheat. But I have prayed for you, Simon, that your faith may not fail. And when you have turned back, strengthen your brothers."

I needed to grow mentally and emotionally. Inadequacy and anxiety not only interfered in my life, but could influence my effectiveness in my work. I understood this during the licensing exam process. Painful as it was, I needed to walk through difficulties and overcome them, not try to escape them. His grace is sufficient, and

His hand holds us as we walk through, rather than fly over, our difficulties.

Jesus, my anchor, prayed my faith would not fail. I knew my anchor held me steady through rough waters and unexpected swells. Yet, we dare not forget it is through Jesus we have power. He desires to do abundantly more than we could ever dare to believe – above our highest prayers. To God be the glory.

PART TWO.
COME WHAT MAY

Chapter Eight

Stay Close to Me

In November 2002, I traveled to the University of the Nations, (part of YWAM) in Hawaii for a conference on Whole Person Ministry. During this time, YWAM and Mercy Ships were making strategic decisions about the future relationship between the organizations. While it made good business and legal sense for the two organizations to be relationally but not legally connected, it caused pain for many who had been part of both for over twenty years.

I joined a small group from YWAM and Mercy Ships who went to pray on the YWAM property. One of the women said, "You need to stand under that tree! The presence of God is so strong!" I walked swiftly to the tree with childlike faith. As promised, I felt enveloped by God—the sweet, safe, loving presence saturated me. Swaying branches, colorful with breadth and depth, gently lulled me near sleep. I was nestled under His wings in His everlasting arms. I imagined the rest of my life in this powerfully peaceful space in time.

Settling in, a few Scriptures came to mind. Jeremiah 17:7-8 reminds us that as we trust in the Lord, we become like trees planted by the water which have no fear or worries and continue to bear fruit. And Psalm 91:14-16 reads, "'Because he loves me,' says the Lord, 'I will rescue him; I will protect him, for he acknowledges my name. He will call on me, and I will answer him; I will be with him in trouble, I will deliver him and honor him and show him my salvation.'"

I pondered those Scriptures, still warmed by the soothing Presence of God. A still, small voice interrupted my journey into heaven. The Holy Spirit whispered, "Stay close to Me." The words perplexed me, because I lingered under the tree for that purpose.

Everyone returned to the group. I shared what the Holy Spirit spoke to me, and one of the leaders asked, "Do you think that is for YWAM and Mercy Ships?"

I said, "I don't think so. I think it is for Jeff and for me." At the time, I was not sure why, but I would soon learn the sobering reason for the word, "Stay close to Me."

Jeff was now a college junior. He hurt his shoulder after lifting weights and playing tennis, so the physician thought he had a ligament injury, based on the history and the nature of the pain. He started Jeff on anti-inflammatory medications, but did not take an x-ray.

While I was at the conference, Jeff was playing the role of King Henry V in a theater performance at his university. England and France were at war, and King Henry V engaged in a sword fight with the King of France. Jeff was in tremendous pain when I talked with him. During worship that night, I saw a vision of Jeff on stage as Henry V, with his right hand holding the sword above his head toward God. Angels were flying all around him. No one else was in the vision. *Thank you, Lord,* I thought. *Jeff will be fine.*

Months passed. Monday morning, May 5th, my devotional calendar read, "The Lord's promises, His plans, His every word stands fast, no matter what news we receive. There is nothing, on earth or in hell or heaven, in time or in eternity, which can alter in any sense what God has promised—because all things serve Him." God caught my attention. I expected negative news. But nothing God promises can be altered since His every word stands.

Jeff called a few hours later, concerned his shoulder pain might be due to something more serious. He was sent for an x-ray and an MRI. I was worried about his health and powerless to do anything about the pain. Jeff's tests indicated an urgent need for him to see a cancer specialist. Jeff said the x-ray showed his bone looked mushy. I made appointments at a respected and well-known cancer center. Cancer seemed an unlikely intruder—but ... what if?

I joined Jeff in West Texas, then we drove seven hours to reach the cancer center before morning. Jeff and his girlfriend Raychel (now his wife) took one car; I drove the other. Jeremiah 17:7-8 came to mind, and I composed a song. "I will not fear when heat comes, and I will not cease bearing fruit. For I will rejoice in Jesus my Savior, my God and my soon coming King." Over and over, I sang—driving through the night.

The surgeon looked carefully at the x-rays. "Jeff has a slow-growing tumor," he said.

I asked, "Does that mean it's not malignant?"

He answered, "No, we can't say that. We need to do biopsies of the tumor."

Jeff and Raychel were joking before the visit, but now things were different. The atmosphere changed from nervous laughter to stunned silence as we considered the ominous journey before us.

Jeff winced with pain from the biopsies—a result of being under-anesthetized, coupled with pain from the tumor. The three of us returned home, waiting for the surgeon, pathologist, and oncologist to discuss the results and plan the next steps.

A sudden and violent storm came with lightning, hail, and thunder during a prayer meeting. I remembered Psalm 18:1-18, where David called for help as the snares of death confronted him. The Lord was angry, and smoke came from His nostrils. He rescued David from his powerful enemy, who was too strong for him, with bolts of lightning. He reached down from on high and drew him out of deep waters. It's not often a thunderstorm is comforting, but that night I knew God heard our prayers and was moving in the heavenly realm on Jeff's behalf. I stood convinced of God's concern and sovereignty. I drove home in peace.

The next day, the surgeon called with results. He said, "The biopsy was inconclusive. We disagree whether the tumor is malignant. The safest course of action is to start six months of chemotherapy as soon as possible. If we take out the tumor before starting chemo and it's malignant, we won't know if the chemo is effective because we won't be able to measure its growth. We need to get Jeff started with the oncologist and the treatment right away." My heart sank. The potential diagnosis was osteosarcoma, a lethal cancer which often takes life or results in amputation of a limb. Reluctantly—prayerfully—I called Jeff. Regardless of the tumor's malignancy, we faced several challenging and life-altering months. We needed our Rock—our Fortress—our Healer—our Deliverer—our Savior.

Our worlds turned upside down, and the new normal disrupted all areas of our lives. We dropped everything to make plans for a 6–12-month stay near the cancer center. My friends held one more prayer gathering on Memorial Day, just before the three of us prepared to leave. I grabbed necessities for an undetermined time away from my home and Mercy Ships, and Jeff packed hastily, not sure how this detour might affect his education. Countless questions and concerns bombarded our minds.

The day to start chemotherapy arrived. Time stood still when this paradoxical life-giving, yet destructive substance slithered down the tube into Jeff's body. I knew about chemo since I was a nurse. But watching Jeff being hooked up to such caustic chemicals was personal. This was my son. This was Jeff's life. Is chemo painful? Was it worth it? Would he live? The road ahead loomed before us with potential pitfalls.

The oncologist insisted we move within 3 miles of the hospital, since Jeff's immune-compromised condition could be life-threatening. Through Mercy Ships and YWAM connections, we learned of a couple living close to the hospital with an available cottage. They offered us their cottage at no cost—for as long as we needed it. Their faith, their generosity, and their love continue to fortify me in my life and work. They knew Jeff might not live. Their commitment to stand by us, no matter what, solidified our relationship. The Body of Christ, serving together—at any cost.

Jeff spent his 21st birthday in the hospital, surrounded by close friends—not what any of us expected for a birthday celebration. All of us were struck by how pale, how thin, how bald he was. Yet Jeff was alive. Our friends stood with us without wavering.

We were grateful but spent. Despite two months of treatment, the tumor grew twice its size, which caused increased pain. The medical team made the right decision when they started chemo first, since tumor removal prior to treatment meant tumor growth could not be measured. The oncologist changed the type of chemo, and three additional months of treatment were planned prior to surgery.

Jeff purposed to ask Raychel to marry him in the middle of this crisis. My heart broke for him. What humility it took to surrender his strength, his masculinity, and even his excitement. *Did he question whether he would live long enough to get married? If he lived, how might the cancer limit not only physical ability, but career choices? What if Raychel chose not to marry him?*

Jeff crawled out of bed and on one knee asked Raychel to marry him after an underwhelming macaroni and cheese dinner. It was not the "event" either of them dreamed of for a marriage proposal. Jeff might die or live a physically compromised life. I thank God Raychel said "Yes." Jeff was stronger with Raychel by his side.

Close friends continued to visit and sat with Jeff so I could take a break. I struggled tremendously. I could not pray, and had trouble reading, which made me angry and disappointed in myself. I thought, *I am being hit from all sides. How can I help others when all I want to do is cry? I should be stronger than this.* I remembered the Scripture Isaiah 49:23b, "Then you will know that I am the Lord; those who hope in me will not be disappointed." Faith is believing in God. Not the outcomes. I share this Scripture with others but could not lean into it myself. I needed to regroup, but felt physically, mentally, and emotionally drained. Depression lurked. Having experienced it before, I knew the warning signs.

In September, a friend invited me to a silent retreat. I did not want to talk, and being away from the life-threatening event, the pain, and the stress provided a welcome pause. My sense of powerlessness crippled me. My room number was 29, and I remembered Psalm 29:10-11 which reads, "The Lord sits enthroned over the flood; the Lord is enthroned as King forever. The Lord gives strength to his people; the Lord blesses his people with peace." I returned to my room and read for hours, and God communicated with me in a variety of ways. He knew what words and avenues would draw me near to Him.

Don Stephens recommended I read *God at War*, a book written by Gregory Boyd which confronts the painstaking journey of suffering. God is good, no matter the reasons for suffering. Whether Jeff's cancer was due to the human condition or to a spiritual attack, I must fight a spiritual battle and center myself on God's goodness. Passion stirred. *How did I forget?* Despair paralyzes; faith and hope energize.

I listened as hospital staff called patient numbers during a laboratory visit. While I was shocked people were reduced to numbers, more disheartening was the realization that 55,000 new patients were scheduled for lab work since we arrived at the hospital at the end of May. In a vision, I saw rows of emaciated cancer victims walking slowly over a cliff. Row by row, they moved with emotionless faces, seemingly resigned to their fate. They resembled concentration camp victims, being led to their death. The Holy Spirit said to me, "Fight." Jeff's outcome was uncertain, but I could still make a difference. From that day forward, I walked and prayed for the myriads of cancer patients globally. This gave me purpose. And every day was one day closer to Jeff's surgery.

My Bible reading on October 5th was Joel 2:25-26 (AMPC) "And I will restore or replace for you the years that the locust has eaten … And you shall eat in plenty and be satisfied and praise the name of the Lord your God, who has dealt wonderfully with you. And My people shall never be put to shame."

I prayed for restoration rather than replacement of Jeff's arm but heard a sobering word during the night. "You must see this through to its perfect end." It reminded me of Abraham the night God warned him of impending destruction. Yet He also promised Abraham numerous descendants, comparable to the sands in the sea. I understood victory hovered around the corner— "in the end" —whatever form it took and whenever this cancer journey ended. We are soldiers fighting in a war. And there are casualties.

I have a lifelong love for dolls. Pretending to be a doll, your life can be whatever you want it to be. You dress her up; build her house; decide how, where and with whom she will spend her life. You create a safe and loving environment, even when bad things happen. There was one doll I wanted for Christmas when I was ten years old. In the movie *Pollyanna*, the character experienced trauma, yet saw the bright side—the sweet side of life. I wanted to be like Pollyanna.

The Pollyanna doll was in high demand, and I wanted one desperately. I knew my single-parent mother had little money, but I dared to believe Pollyanna could be mine. On Christmas, there she was, hidden behind the tree, in a huge box wrapped in white tissue paper with my name spelled in bright red tape. Pollyanna was an answer to prayer.

Most of my childhood treasures were lost over the years, but I remembered Pollyanna while praying for Jeff's surgery and bid for her on eBay. The doll would be a tangible expression of God's faithfulness during this dark time. I learned Pollyanna was mine the morning I read Joel 2:24-26. The doll meant so much more to me than a resurfaced childhood memory. Though just a doll, God used this to confirm He heard my prayers. My Father knows how to draw me close. To anyone—to me—a prayer answered in secret declares the greatness of God.

The surgeon scheduled Jeff's operation for November 11th, and I needed strength to stand beside Jeff and Raychel. I chose to fast and pray without ceasing until surgery. I walked on the beach in Galveston and said, "Lord, I'm here. I wait to hear from you." For hours I walked near the shore, waiting and listening. Some thoughts frightened me, destabilized me. I timidly stepped into crashing waves and heard, "Though the enemy comes in like a flood, the Spirit of the Lord raises up a standard against him." Fear overwhelmed me. *Might the enemy flood us with death and destruction?* Though shaken, I stood firm in the water, trusting God's standard, His Spirit. He promised peace and deliverance.

I grew more confident that God heard me and was deeply involved in the situation. The Holy Spirit said, "Daughter, did I not tell you and promise you that if you believe and rely on Me, you shall see the Glory of God? Dare to believe." I sensed all of heaven watching me as I stood on the beach, standing fast on God's faithfulness. I knew God and His heavenly host loved my dependence on the power of the blood of Jesus.

November 11th, Veterans Day—surgery day. Jeff, Raychel and I and several others met at the hospital. I struggled to sit still, expecting a long and arduous day. I had no idea what Scripture to read to give me peace and comfort. In desperation, I opened my Bible, trusting God for a seemingly random but deliberate Scripture. I longed for a fresh and faith-solidifying word.

I opened the Bible to Joshua 10, which shared how God annihilated the enemy as the people went forth in battle. God defeated the enemy in a single campaign. He went before Joshua and the

Israelites in battle, leaving no survivors. My faith grew. Every time hospital staff gave us new information, my friend and I circled the hospital, praying. Jesus annihilates the enemy; no cancer cell would survive. I was now certain of it. Jeff came out of surgery twelve hours later, after the surgeon successfully inserted the donor bone and the titanium shoulder joint into Jeff's body. Now we must wait for the outcome. I thanked God for choosing a wise, patient, and compassionate surgeon. His quiet, loving confidence settled the angst in the atmosphere.

Jeff was discharged amid a major storm. A few hours later, Jeff's temperature inched its way above 100 degrees. *Here we go again, Father.* Another life-threatening event, so soon. I left to get the car ready before taking Jeff out in the rain and found it partially submerged in water. I determinedly drove to the hospital, and the staff managed the life-threatening symptoms. Truly, the enemy attacked with raging waters and threatened to overwhelm us. We fought a relentless battle, but God raised up a standard against the foe.

Though Jeff experienced physical trauma, we all experienced emotional trauma. My stamina dissipated. Trudging through the mire with Jeff and Raychel caused more pain than the trauma from my past. My world teetered on a precipice, though I considered myself a woman of gripping faith. Watching my only son in debilitating pain, unable to stand, fighting countless infections, unnerved me. Would that I had cancer instead of Jeff. But twelve years of solid faith proved my Heavenly Father loved, saved, and delivered. Even so, I cried, "Turn to me and be gracious to me; give your strength to your servant, and save the son of your maidservant." (Psalm 86:16, ESV). My cries were not completely self-serving. I needed to be strong for all three of us.

God met me each day, whether through prayer, worship, daily walks, or all three at the same time. I knew He was near. He spoke to me. God was my fortress, Scripture my rampart and bulwark. Psalm 18:28-30: "You, Lord, keep my lamp burning; my God turns my darkness into light. With your help I can run against a troop; with my God I can scale a wall. As for God, his way is perfect: The Lord's word is flawless; he shields all who take refuge in him." Yes, His way is perfect.

Jesus was ever-present and so was the body of Christ. Support came through family, friends, and people I didn't know during Jeff's treatment. People sat with us at the hospital. Others came to repair the computer. Friends took me to lunch. Some sent words of encouragement. Many sent us money, and two people sent us cars. People made room in their homes for us. Instructors gave Jeff a leave of absence. Raychel's parents allowed her to move near us during Jeff's treatment and postpone graduation for six months. Mercy Ships gave me time away to stay with Jeff. Countless people prayed. The Body of Christ stood in the gap and lifted our arms.

Ezekiel 37 was the focus of my daily prayer walks, that Jeff's bone would develop a blood supply, with no further infections. It would take several weeks to get the surgical biopsy results. Clear margins give greater assurance no cancer remains. Six weeks later, results showed clear margins, but only 85 percent of the tumor died, which meant Jeff required six more months of chemo. With sixteen hospitalizations in one year, he spent more time in the hospital than at home.

Jeff ended the cancer journey with his final chemo treatment on Memorial Day. Most people think finishing treatment is a time to celebrate, unaware that grief is a process and does not end with a single event. Though spent, we were desperate to resume abundant living. Jeff and Raychel drove to West Texas, while a friend and I drove back to Mercy Ships. We saw it through to its perfect end. God walked with us every step of the way.

The devotional I read, May 5, 2003, prepared me for the long road ahead. "The Lord's promises, His plans, His every word stands fast, no matter what news we receive. There is nothing, on earth or in hell or heaven, in time or in eternity, which can alter in any sense what God has promised – because all things serve Him."

Amen. So be it.

Chapter Nine

God of the Impossible

On several occasions, I received confirmation that I was to be ordained as a minister. It seemed illogical and a highly improbable possibility. Who would recommend someone like me to become a minister of the gospel? I doubted anyone would take me seriously since I was divorced and a woman. I recoiled in horror and disbelief each time I thought of ordination. Is this the angel of light speaking to me? How do I know this is God speaking? I kept those thoughts to myself for years.

My denomination did not ordain people who were divorced, evidence I pursued an impossible dream. I wrote a letter to the denominational headquarters about divorced people being considered for ordination and received a discouraging response. My head dropped as I read the letter. The Holy Spirit said, "Traditions of men make the gospel of no effect." I needed to regroup, so I pushed thoughts of ordination out of my mind and retreated into my shell.

A short time later, my pastor, Ken Cramer, handed me a packet of information and an application for the International Ministerial Fellowship (IMF). The organization considers and credentials people for ministry at various levels. He said, "Contact these people." An atomic seed of hope sprouted.

A few years later, I spoke with one of the DTS leaders about ordination, and he, too, recommended IMF, since a prominent YWAM leader sat on the nominating and acceptance committee. Ordination through an international and interdenominational fellowship opened more doors than one representing a specific faith group. I considered his comments since I hoped to serve internationally.

Ordination came up often after I transferred to chaplaincy in Mercy Ships, and I spoke with the senior chaplain about the process. He asked, "What could you do if ordained you cannot do now?"

I said, "There's nothing required for my job I don't have, but I believe God is directing me toward ordination."

He said, "Do you think it's to help Pharisees understand God's compassion?"

"No", I answered. "I believe God wants people like me, people with a disastrous past to know His love, acceptance, and that nothing is irredeemable."

He saves to the uttermost. He knows the end from the beginning. He already knew our choices and the purpose for our lives includes those choices.

After a decade of confirmation, it was time to revisit ordination. My life was virtually on hold during the year Jeff was in treatment, which allowed me time to consider and pray about the future. I paradoxically desired and dreaded ordination. I believed God prompted me to pursue it. Honestly, it was easier to stay in my role as a lay chaplain than confront the scrutiny of people who believed different theology. Would I humiliate myself? Would I disparage Mercy Ships? After all, I did not "need" it to serve as a missionary, mental health professional, educator, or chaplain. Yet, thoughts of ordination surfaced more often and with greater urgency.

I asked Deyon if she and Don would recommend me for ordination. She said, "Yes, and we can have the service at our house."

I said, "You would recommend me, even with my history?"

Deyon said, "Especially because of your history."

I am extremely grateful for the people God put into my life. Deyon, a role model and close friend since I came to Mercy Ships, inspired me to go deeper into God and to persevere through adversity. Her compassion, ability to see into the spiritual realm, fervent prayer, and her wisdom and knowledge of Scripture challenge me to grow.

I went to lunch with a friend not long after. She said, "Oh look, there's Don Stephens and Leland Paris." Leland was the director of the Twin Oaks YWAM base. I nodded as we walked by, since I did not want to disturb them. Don stopped me and said, "Leland, this is who I just told you about. Deyon and I would like you to recommend her for ordination." God made the connection, and I began the paperwork process.

My pastor wrote a recommendation, as did the previous international chaplain for Mercy Ships. After I submitted my application, IMF staff called to set up an interview with one of the senior pastors. My thoughts raced. *He read my history. What does he think of me? What questions will he ask?* My frequent companions of fear, shame, and inadequacy smothered me. But nothing ventured, nothing gained. Jesus suffered humiliation on the cross. I could do the same.

The interviewing pastor listened intently and kindly to my story. I answered his questions, and rather than humiliating me, he encouraged me. I learned the team of pastors approved my application for ordination. A few months later, Leland led the ordination service at Don and Deyon's home, Jeff led worship, and several friends were present. I knew that those who participated supported me wholeheartedly. Honored and humbled, I prayed God would bless this step and increase His kingdom through me.

Years later, the denomination changed their doctrine and allowed divorced people to seek ordination. Countless denominations exist in the world, and no two agree on everything. The common denominator is the gospel message. Did Jesus die for our sins? Are all things possible with God? Did God create all people in His image? Are all people created equal? Are we new creatures—the old has passed away, and the new has come? Will people see me as I am or as I was? Scripture declares you will know them by their fruit. Does my life, my fruit, look different than it did thirty years ago? Ultimately, God is my judge. No one stands before Him in my place. Except Jesus.

Not long after, I wrote to my supporters to share the news. Most sent congratulations and gave words of hope and wisdom. One church withdrew prayer and financial support. When I asked the reason, I learned they withdrew support because I was a woman, not because I was divorced. Leadership believed women could be in ministry, but not as licensed or ordained ministers. In some ways, their answer gave me peace, even though the experience was painful. I am responsible for my life choices. I am not responsible for being born a woman.

The church provided the bulk of my funding at that time; withdrawing support left me in a precarious financial position. But God is my provider, not the church. God owns everything and can distribute as He sees fit. I knew He would provide, though I couldn't see how. A few months later, someone started supporting me at the same level as the church. The funds came from a single woman with an average salary from the same state, unsolicited, and unaware of the battle. I know her sacrifice, the desires of her heart, and I know God is faithful. May I be found faithful doing the work of the Father—believing in the One He has sent; and remain steadfast as a handmaiden whose bonds have been loosed as I sit at His feet. And may she be rewarded one hundred-fold for continuing to support the ministry God has given me.

There were times when I thought God was late in meeting my needs, but He never was. It's difficult to fathom the stress of raising support if you have never done so. Everyone lives by faith, but depending on God to provide without a predictable paycheck creates internal and external conflicts. The amount people give is not my concern. What He asks of me is to be grateful and generous.

The people who keep me on the field through prayer, giving, and love are my heroes. They stand in the gap; they lift my arms, and I call each one friend. God has been my provider for over twenty-five years of full-time missions. "Your prosperity will not come from a man," He said, shortly before Jeff and I began the life-changing drive in 1996.

Chapter Ten

Moving on Board

I was thrilled to return to Mercy Ships after Jeff finished cancer treatment. I took a deep breath, then stepped into my new home, a cottage by a lake. No more chemo. No new infections. No debilitating physical or emotional pain. I thanked God for a season of fresh opportunity.

Jeff and Raychel completed their wedding plans, and others planned showers. The wedding was small but meaningful, followed by a reception at Mercy Ships. Jeff sang a love song he wrote to Raychel. Many shed tears—tears of joy and tears of relief that Jeff had survived his near-death experience with cancer.

I accepted a short-term assignment as an onboard chaplain, and flew to chilly Bremerhaven, Germany, to join the *Anastasis* crew. But living out your dream doesn't mean everything is perfect. The ship's pipes broke, and icy cold water gave me brain freeze when I showered. The *Anastasis* was old, but faithful. Just like the ship, faithfulness, rather than comfort, motivates the crew.

Because of unusually rough seas, we sailed toward Tenerife, Canary Islands, with the bow roped off. Powerful, majestic waves danced before my porthole. The ship rocked to and fro, back and forth. Pitch and roll. Heavy equipment in the galley and on the deck crashed against the sides. We secured everything, but large items broke the restraints. The aging but determined *Anastasis* pushed her way forward as we trusted this precious old ship to carry us southward to serve the world's poor.

Jeff called me and said he had chest pain. I knew chemo caused physical symptoms, cardiac being one of them, so I told him to go to the emergency room. I thought, *What in the world am I doing here? Out in the middle of the ocean, and I'm powerless. What was I thinking?* Jeff called again, but with a calm voice. Not to worry, since his symptoms had resulted from panic, rather than a medical emergency. After a life-threatening illness, every symptom stirs up terrible possibilities for survivors and those closest to them. *Thank you, Father. Thank you for watching over us.*

I loved the time in Tenerife, and the frigid days in Bremerhaven faded amid warm, sunny weather. I savored memories of the visit Jeff and I took in 2000 after he graduated from high school. So much had happened since then. Spending time in the shipyard allowed for great balance between serving the crew, fitting into my new role, and sightseeing. Soon we sailed off for Benin, a country in West Africa.

In early November, we held a screening to decide which patients could be treated surgically. I did not anticipate the number of people or the desperation they experienced. Hundreds waited patiently in line each day, hoping Mercy Ships could meet their needs and heal their devastated bodies. Facial tumors, cleft lip and palate, orthopedic deformities, blindness, and other anomalies crippled the lives of those who inched their way forward.

All the crew played some part and did so with never-ceasing compassion. Some served water to those in line. Others provided security. Many played games with the children, who came either as patients or to accompany their parents. I joined the prayer team to pray for people who did not have a surgical solution. Yes, we have medical professionals, but ultimately, healing comes from Jesus.

The Advent season flew by, filled with festivities for patients and crew. How rich to share the birth of Jesus with 350 people from more than 35 nations, as culture blended with spiritual truths in a unique and meaningful way. After the Christmas Eve service, the crew scurried around the ship, depositing little gifts in shoes left outside each cabin. This is a European tradition, in honor of St. Nicholas. On Christmas morning, crew members opened their cabin doors and found their shoes overflowing with simple treasures.

I agreed to transfer permanently to the *Anastasis*, but when an earthquake and tsunami devastated the Indian Ocean coastline on December 26th, 2004, I questioned my decision. The earthquake measured a staggering 9.1–9.3 on the Richter scale, and 227,898 people died. So many lives lost—lives changed—in an instant. Memories of Nicaragua stirred my passion. Serving on the ship, far from the devastation, I wondered if my future included disaster response. Not today, but one day.

We set sail for a shipyard in East London, South Africa, after the Benin field service ended. Since most crew go home after field service, those remaining share the workload. Families move off the ship, and single crew members stay to serve in whatever way needed. I loved standing fire watch. Welding occasionally drops sparks, which may land and slowly smolder. One night, as I sat alone in the dark worshipping, I could smell and see smoke. The fire team responded to my call, preventing a fire. No job is unimportant.

The *Anastasis,* originally named the *Victoria*, was an exquisitely and ornately decorated Italian passenger ocean liner built in 1953. She was a beautiful lady, decked with expensive silver and porcelain dishes. One of my favorite locations was the double spiral staircase that whimsically wound down from one level to the main deck. Mercy Ships purchased this rare beauty and refit her as a hospital ship. She served well for decades.

But life-changing news interrupted the peace and tranquility of the crew. The *Anastasis* would be decommissioned. Logically, the decision made sense. In a few years, the *Anastasis* would not meet maritime requirements, primarily because of its large amount of wood, which was now considered a fire risk. If remodeling a ship was not an option due to the cost, decommissioning or destruction followed. It was decided the *Anastasis* would be scrapped once the *Africa Mercy* was fully transformed from a rail ferry into a hospital ship in Newcastle, England.

Decommissioning the ship was complicated, and required wise, effective leadership, combined with prayer. Each Mercy Ship is more than a physical structure and embodies every person who serves as a living stone in the Body of Christ. When I left for the *Anastasis*, I expected to live on board her for years. I expected to serve alongside the managing director I already knew. I had no idea the *Anastasis* was slated for the salvage yard.

Having moved so many times in my life, I had little understanding of the upheaval it created in the lives of those who had lived on board for twenty years or more. My own expectations and the expectations of others upset my plan as well. *Was I prepared to navigate these changes? How will the crew respond? Would I have the capacity as head chaplain to lead others through the journey of grief they were destined to experience?* A guest speaker on board said, "Those who love much, grieve much." Many grieved much. Short-term crew, long-term crew, from the youngest to the oldest, would each react differently to the decision.

I trusted leadership, yet wondered what my future held. My response to the decision and to the looming responsibilities I carried was to begin a liquid fast for forty days, with fervent prayer. I knew my next steps required God's wisdom and not my own. In scripture, Proverbs 3:5-6 reads, "Trust in the Lord with all your heart and lean not on your own understanding; in all your ways submit to him, and he will make your paths straight."

Yes, Lord. I submit my ways. I wholeheartedly acknowledge what lies ahead is beyond my limited abilities. Please take the helm.

The crew received several tickets for a teleconference offered through Willow Creek, a mega church near Chicago. *Please God, I prayed. Give me direction. I want to follow You, not my own plan.* During the initial prayer, the Holy Spirit repeated something He spoke to me years ago. I tuned out the person leading prayer, as God gave me a personal and specific word: "Don't get lost with the saved," He said. The word, in the past and at this juncture, meant my mission is not only to those who know Jesus, but to serve those who don't. My primary mandate is to build the kingdom, rather than encourage and equip the Church. *Today I must listen.*

Bill Hybels, (then senior pastor of Willow Creek) said vision is preceded by the capacity for activism. "God's heart and the human heart are joined in what frustrates ... What breaks your heart? Whatever breaks your heart breaks the heart of God. That is what you are called to do ... Surrender your ego because the cause is more important ... take risks you would not normally take ... the sense of urgency enables you." Though Bill Hybels is no longer leading Willow Creek, I am reminded we are imperfect people living in an imperfect world. God redeems imperfect people—like me. I was impacted by Bill's message, and expectant for what might lie ahead.

The next speaker, Rick Warren, talked about Moses and how God led him. Moses had a wooden shepherd's staff. God told Moses if he laid down his staff, then picked it up again, it would carry the power of God. Rick Warren said the staff we need to lay down includes income, identity and influence: "If you lay it down, God will make it come alive in ways you could not imagine."

I knew what to do; return to Texas after the decommissioning of the ship. I would do whatever I could to implement disaster response services in Mercy Ships. I had already surrendered income; now I must surrender identity and influence as a chaplain. And this required further risk. What if I gave up chaplaincy and had nowhere to go? Yet I would lay down my staff, come what may. Ultimately, there is no risk in responding when God speaks.

From East London we sailed to Cape Town, with a backdrop of whales, Table Mountain, and Lion's Head. More than 17,000 people toured the ship in just a few weeks to learn more about the work we do. Tours also led to new volunteers and donations. I learned a valuable lesson while having my hair done in the ship salon. A large group of visitors filed past the salon, peering inside and taking photos. I was unnerved by the violation of my privacy, and immediately aware people in the countries where we serve often experience the same intrusion. So often, we are unaware of how our behavior affects others.

At the end of October 2005, we packed for and sailed to Liberia to begin field service. United Nations Military (UNMIL) peacekeepers lined the dock, a striking contrast to docking in Cape Town. Security remained a concern, as the nation emerged from fourteen years of civil war. Cape Town and Liberia, though on the same continent, are as different as night and day.

I struggled with people's overwhelming needs. They had nothing after the war. Lack of food, housing, and medical services, coupled by grief, seemed insurmountable. No domestic animals remained, only bush meat. Prices skyrocketed and Liberians could no longer afford to buy rice, their staple food. Research indicated 44 percent of the population experienced trauma, which manifested in depression, post-traumatic stress disorder, substance use disorder, and, in some cases, severe mental disorders.

Many people approached me with demands while I prayer walked on the dock.

"You need to get me inside."

"You need to give me money for food."

"You need to give me money to pay the hospital bill so my wife and baby can come home."

I was not prepared for the desperation of war-torn Liberians, since my previous experiences in Bosnia and Sierra Leone were part of a small team, not a massive medical ship. Overwhelmed, I prayed God would help me cope. Immediately, as I passed a security guard, he said, "I need a Bible." God knew just what to do to—He used my love of Scripture and leading people to Jesus to stir my passion to meet a need.

The crew took an offering and purchased 600 Bibles from the local Bible Society. The ship's security officer and I signed and handed them out to all who came. Two Nepali soldiers came to get a Bible. It could be death to them, yet they took the risk. Many people from higher income countries live with religious freedom. People from countries without such freedom are willing to die for it.

I've worked for many years with the US military and have a special attachment for servicemen and women and their families. I prayed, "Father, I would love to get a photo of soldiers lined up for a Bible." God did better than that. A group of 20–30 UNMIL soldiers came to the ship in formation, in uniform, with guns over their shoulders, singing praise songs. God loves to answer prayers. Later, the Chaplain from the Ghanaian detachment wrote, "We strongly believe that our commitment to the reading of these Bibles and articulating the message it carries to our lives, will immensely enhance our lives as Christians. It will also help us in our profession as soldiers of peace and ultimately lead us to salvation."

The eight-month field service was packed with purpose. Volunteer crew provided surgical and medical care; built bridges, schools, and churches; planted gardens in prisons, orphanages, and villages; empowered teachers; trained facilitators in adult literacy; and rebuilt the water treatment plant in Monrovia. When field service ended, thousands of lives had been changed forever.

Decommissioning of the *Anastasis* was slower than planned as the *Africa Mercy* refit was delayed. This decommissioned Danish ferry had sailed for years between Scandinavian countries, with people, supplies, cars, and trains onboard. Shipyard bankruptcy was the primary cause of the delay, and it capsized many people's plans. Some were angry; some were grateful. I agreed to stay until November to help with the transition—but no later.

The overwhelming needs of the people, and my inability to meet them, nearly hardened my heart. We risk missing the miracle when this happens, and purpose is clouded. In Mark 6, Jesus promised His disciples rest in a desolate place. Intense ministry and grief over the beheading of John the Baptist drained them. But when they arrived, over 5,000 people were there, all needing food. Jesus provided food for all, but it required effort from the disciples to organize and feed the people. Then they sailed to the other side of the lake, with no break, and faced terrifying and overwhelming sea conditions on the way. They developed hardened hearts due to overload and unmet expectations.

Perhaps God shows us the part of the plan our level of faith can handle. If we knew the entire journey ahead, we may recoil in horror. We might not go at all. If I knew the *Anastasis* had just a few years left to serve, I might not have made such a major move. It does not mean we made the wrong decision because the outcomes change.

The road had constant detours, yet they led me to where God wanted me. As a newcomer on board, I brought fresh perspective without the same level of grief as those who served for years. This made me more objective and more effective than if I faced the same loss as the hundreds of people surrounding me. Though part of the path was hidden, God had a plan for me. Proverbs 16:3 says, "Commit to the Lord whatever you do, and he will establish your plans."

Chapter Eleven

The Mental Health Program Begins

During the field service in Liberia in 2005, the Liberian Minister of Health approached Mercy Ships and requested psychosocial care as a part of the field service projects upon our return in 2007. This meant we could provide mental health care not only for crew, but for the nations. A sea of need appeared before us. Liberia, a nation ravaged by fourteen years of civil war, had only one psychiatrist and one psychologist.

The Vice President of International Programs asked me to accept the responsibility of providing psychosocial care, which answered my decades-long prayer. Years of study and walking alongside people prepared me for this, and I had glimpses of this reality during my short trips to Bosnia and Nicaragua. But—I had conflicting motivations. On the one hand, this was my opportunity to "not get lost with the saved." Yet it seemed an impossible task, and I wondered how I could start this project in a nation with only two national mental health professionals and approximately six months to develop the program. I walked into the laundry room on the ship and saw a poster on the office door: "Jesus is only one man." *Yes, Lord. I am only one woman, but you are always with me.*

My God-given purpose for the nations focused on bringing healing to people and building mental health capacity. It's wonderful to help individuals heal, but if there is no path forward for healing others in the future, the work accomplished is limited in scope. This combination of direct intervention and capacity building provides a structure for lasting development around mental health services. Mercy Ships projects are offered in low- and middle-income countries, and unfortunately mental health is an area of health care more underserved than others.

Some countries are devastated by war or conflict; others are decimated by diseases. A common thread is that all of them experience high levels of trauma or grief, often both, and the population overall has nowhere to process the deep pain that may lie dormant for years. It is uncommon for people in most nations to share their stories with others, but even if they want to, there often isn't a safe person to share them with.

I returned to the International Support Center in Texas in the fall of 2006 after serving eighteen months on board. Settling into both Chaplaincy and Health Care Services, I resumed member care for the staff and began designing the mental health program. While the Government of Liberia requested training for primary health care workers, as a minister I hoped to equip church leaders as well. Working with the vice-president of Programs and the national mental health coordinator in Liberia, we reached an agreement to include church leaders. Adding another service provider group increased our ability to impact the nation at multiple levels.

Initial content development included materials written by Summer Institute of Linguistics (SIL) and Wycliffe Bible Translators (Wycliffe), besides the adapted Maslow's Hierarchy of Needs, the Whole Person Model, the Behavior Process Model, and the Change Model. These models assist in both learning the story and seeking direction in guiding the individual, family, or group toward healing.

Whole person is a common term for considering all aspects of an individual's life when learning their story. The physical body, the soul, the spirit, and social relationships assist the service provider in identifying in which area the primary problem originates, and how each area is affected. Drs. Dan Fountain and Sherry O'Donnell designed a similar image, used by both medical and non-medical workers alike.

The Behavior Process Model answers the question of why people do what they do by identifying: 1) the situation; 2) the thoughts; 3) the feelings; and 4) the behavior. Thoughts are the most important part of the model, since they affect both feelings and behavior.

Positive thoughts lead to positive behavior, and negative thoughts lead to negative behavior.

There are many theories on the change process, but I have developed a model that is quite simple to understand. The model has five parts, which include: 1) awareness; 2) motivation; 3) knowledge and skills; 4) energy; and 5) hope. People may become stuck at any level, but the most serious level is a lack of hope. Hopelessness may lead to serious consequences, such as suicide.

Program design continued despite the fact both Jeff and I faced physical complications. In early 2007, Jeff developed excruciating pain because of tendons and ligaments disconnecting from the donor bone in his right arm post-cancer. Jeff had been a worship leader and played acoustic guitar since he was fifteen years old, and this sudden injury threatened his ability to play. An internal injury is not visible to others, and as a result, many people have little tolerance for those who have limited mobility. This increased pressure on Jeff and, as a mother, increased my stress as well.

A few months later, I woke in the night light-headed, as if my heart had stopped beating. I fell to the floor and thought I might die. My roommate called 911, and I spent the night in the emergency room. Decommissioning of the ship, debriefing crew members and their children, the transition home, and Jeff's physical crisis caused stress and added to a genetic predisposition toward arrhythmia. My physician recommended I take a month away from work, after which I was cleared for travel since the arrhythmia was not life-threatening.

I returned to Liberia in June 2007 in time for the transfer of crew from the *Anastasis* to the *Africa Mercy*. The *Anastasis* would soon be laid to rest, with many mourning the loss of this faithful old ship—the Mercy Ships flagship. Yes, life is bittersweet, just like the cross. We mourn the loss of life as we knew it yet have hope for what lies ahead. I considered the compounding effect of multiple significant stressors in my own life and knew I must pace myself going forward.

At the government's request, I served two days a week at a rural health clinic in one village, and two more days training multi-denominational church leaders in basic assessment and counseling in the capital city of Monrovia.

The beginning of the program was both physically and mentally taxing as I worked alone and drove myself to the venues. Carrying buckets of food, driving to and from the venue, and doing all the training exhausted me.

Some days the galley crew forgot to make food, so I quickly prepared sandwiches for the participants. There weren't designated funds for mental health since it was a pioneer program. I hesitated to ask for resources, either financial or human, since the program had been launched as a trial, but I knew it was physically impossible for me to continue working alone. I asked leadership for a driver on the days I carried food, and they agreed. I didn't think to ask sooner due to my blessing (or curse) of self-sufficiency. On clinic days, I drove alone and enjoyed the 1 ½–2-hour drive through markets and tropical foliage.

Monrovia, Liberia, is one of the wettest cities in the world, and it floods during the rainy season. I never liked rain, so unless I chose to think differently, the next few months would be miserable. When I walked down the gangway the first morning, I said, "Thank you, Lord, for the rain." I stepped into water above my shoes, then drove the Land Rover through high water and mud. I learned to shout above the sound of rain pounding on a tin roof during training. My attitude improved as I realized temperatures were cooler during the rainy season, and I became better at thanking God in all circumstances.

I absolutely loved my work and the country. Though I wished I had team members, I realized God planned for me to develop the program alone since the project required adjustment every day. I worked with capable and dedicated Liberians, and we learned from each other. I collaborated with the Ministry of Health Mental Health Task Force, which gave me a better understanding of the overwhelming need with nearly nonexistent services.

Health care participants walked for 2 ½ hours through knee-deep water to come for training. One week, church leaders waited for two days when the bridge washed out, missing valuable days working in their fields. The crew gave $1500 for needed medical supplies for the health care clinics where I offered training. Nurses donated their uniforms when they left the ship. Hasbro donated large amounts of Play-Doh for training on counseling with children. Initially, I felt like a pebble in an ocean; but with time, I learned to depend on God as He held all things in His capable hands. People worked together as a living organism, bringing hope and healing.

We heard stories from desperate people who previously suffered in silence. War, poverty, disease, domestic violence, sexual assault, and death during childbirth contribute to loss and grief. How do you comfort parents whose unborn baby died while the mother walked miles to the clinic? For some people, childhood trauma caused deeper pain than living through a 14-year war. Though many stories had similarities, each one was unique.

One young girl, Jane (not her real name), experienced a life-threatening event and was both deaf and mute. Not only did she experience trauma from the event, but she also could not to go to school as there were no resources in the village to help her. Jane stayed on my mind, and I was determined to find a school where she could thrive. My clinic partner and I found a faith-based school for deaf children in Monrovia. Jane was able to live there, go to school, build friendships, and heal from trauma. Her parents were so thankful to know she was in a safe place and finally had opportunities to grow. I experienced personal satisfaction knowing I had made a significant difference in this young girl's life.

The Mental Health Program thrived, and we made plans for the following year when prison workers and teachers working with ex-combatants would also receive training. Projects typically begin in the capital city but then expand deeper into the nation as relationships and understanding of the culture increase. Doors opened quickly, and the Mental Health Program moved forward.

I traveled home to prepare for another Liberia field service in January 2008 and then returned to the *Africa Mercy*. Back in my cabin, I wrote in my journal:

> On the coast of Africa, far from rural villages, we now see streetlights, ride on improved roads, and hear women sweeping streets with brooms provided by the government. Times are changing. There is hope that President Ellen Johnson Sirleaf, the first female president in Africa, will bring the stability and progress this part of Africa longs for.

Funding was provided for 2008, so I was able to include two new team members. Naomi hailed from South Africa, and Torbjoerg, a psychiatrist, served as a short-term team member from Norway. Both have a deep love for Jesus, for Mercy Ships, and for mental health services. Adding them to the team decreased my workload and provided all the benefits that come from a well-functioning team.

Naomi asked me to consider adding a fifth model, the Johari Window, to the workshop content. I realized it fit quite well in the training, since it seeks to identify who is aware of the problem: self, others or both. Johari has four parts which include: 1) arena (what everyone knows); 2) blind spot (what others know about us that we don't know about ourselves; 3) façade (what we know about ourselves, but others don't know); and d) unknown (only God knows what is in the unknown).

Projects continued with a mental health workshop offered at Phoebe Hospital in Gbarnga, where rebel forces attacked in 1994, killing both patients and medical personnel. Graves fill the courtyard to this day as a grim reminder of senseless death.

> Journal entry, March 2008
>
> We just returned from Gbarnga after providing mental health/disorders training for medical officers representing every Liberian county. The national mental health coordinator joined us, and the participants were engaged and humble. They saw so much; worked so hard; and persevered. One of the physicians worked at Phoebe Hospital during the massacre on Sept. 23, 1994. Three staff members were killed, along with 200 patients too sick to run. The physician walked barefoot to Totota, several kilometers away; then delivered a baby for a woman needing a C-section on the road without medication. The woman and baby survived.

Dedicated servants amid traumas.

The Ministry of Health organized a "Stakeholder's Workshop" to initiate developing the country's first National Mental Health Policy. Over seventy national and international participants attended, and I was privileged to be part of national mental health development. Mental health workshops were also held in the interior for 200 providers from various service groups.

As children's grief and trauma healing groups were developed, I was asked to coauthor content for the workshops in partnership with SIL and Wycliffe. We then piloted materials in Uganda and Liberia. Both nations experienced war, so we asked children to write a lament. A lament gives an opportunity to address God and express thoughts and feelings directly.

One child in my small group lamented:

> Oh God why? Why did these things happen to me? I dream about some things. I saw soldiers kill some of my family. I fell on a rock and fell down the stairs. When I do bad things, police carry me

> to jail. I was nearly killed by a car. I was nearly bitten by a snake. But I know you were always there for me. You protected me and saved me. I believe you love me and did not want these bad things to happen to me.

Children, a vulnerable population, suffer unthinkable trauma, primarily due to the behavior of others. I've learned that most children are desperate for a caring person to hear their stories.

Moving into new territory includes new challenges and the likelihood of being blindsided. The father of a child in my children's healing group asked me to take her with me to the US. He told me his new wife was harsh with her, and he wanted her to have a loving home. I was crushed by the story, the question, and the fact that he made the request with the sorrowful girl at his side. It broke my heart to tell them both that I travel constantly for my work, and though I would love to have a little girl, it was not possible. It is difficult to walk the narrow road between guarding your heart and hardening it. To have the heart of Jesus requires a guarded, not hardened heart. The situation also required I work with the organizing church leader to collaborate with the family to improve the dynamics at home for the child.

Situations may or may not change, but the children experience some healing from trauma and learn coping skills to better deal with internal and external stress. On the course evaluation, some parents wrote they would ask forgiveness from their children and discipline and love them in a more positive way.

Pioneering projects is challenging on many levels, and requires enormous amounts of physical, mental, emotional, and social energy. Without a strong spiritual foundation and focused prayer, natural and spiritual battles might sink the program. One endeavor required me to grow in confidence or fail—designing and implementing a counseling program on the radio.

The moderator at Eternal Love Winning Africa (ELWA) and I began "Winds of Hope" with approximately 10,000 listeners. In addition to my daily work, which required training health care workers and church leaders, I accepted the challenge of creating the content and then driving the Land Rover in the dark every Tuesday evening about an hour away from the ship. Some nights another team member or crew member joined me; occasionally, I traveled alone.

Liberia's security was fragile, yet I had peace as I drove. My fear was speaking on the radio to a sea of faceless listeners across Liberia and beyond. Not only did we present topics on mental health, but it was a program where listeners were free to call in with personal situations and questions. In essence, it was a public interview with thousands of traumatized people.

Each week, I or another presenter shared mental health topics, such as trauma, depression, substance misuse, and even bedwetting. Bedwetting is a poorly understood problem, and uninformed parents humiliate or beat children for it. Parents don't intend to be cruel. They just don't know what to do. We emphasize during training that if there is no specific medical problem, bedwetting is most often caused by stress or trauma.

I am convinced the forty-day fast stimulated progress in both purpose and spiritual growth. I drew closer to God as I navigated rocky seas, both natural and spiritual. It opened the door to the future and to favor for the mental health program. Matthew 10:39 reads,

"Whoever finds their life will lose it, and whoever loses their life for my sake will find it." I had clear direction. God's will, not my will, must prevail. Sacrificing my comfort invites me to be a small part of a big thing.

PART THREE.
COUNTING THE COST

Chapter Twelve

Power Struggles

Leviathan frolics in the vast and spacious sea; God laughs as he plays. Perhaps God laughs because Leviathan is powerless in the presence of God.

I grew more comfortable in my role and purpose until a local partner asked me to offer mental health training for church leaders working with ex-combatants. He mentioned Joshua Milton Blahyi, the former "General Butt Naked," who committed horrific atrocities in the Liberian conflict from 1989–1996. I met Joshua in Ghana in 2006 when I served as chaplain. A crew member invited Joshua and his wife on board, and he shared some of his story with a group of crew members.

Meeting a former warlord turned evangelist is not an everyday experience. The war had ended only a few years earlier, and for Liberians serving on board, unhealed wounds remained. Some avoided Joshua; others greeted him. But for many crew members, I saw a mixture of facial reactions. I knew much about the war but little about Joshua and his personal involvement. Overall, I was curious but cautious and wondered whether Joshua was a different man than the one described as the most feared warlord in Liberia. Joshua spoke very little, but greeted crew members, shaking hands with a subdued smile. Before Joshua left, he asked me to pray for him. My spirit was stirred when I prayed for Joshua, and I wondered what it meant. I had not thought about Joshua since his visit to the ship a few years before my project in Liberia began.

I remembered the connection I had previously with Joshua and agreed to include him in our workshop. The partner invited Joshua onboard, and when he came up the gangway, he said with a smile, "I remember you." We talked for some time, and I invited Joshua and other church leaders to join a workshop that would begin in a few months.

I needed additional content to work with ex-combatants and prisoners. A few books I found particularly helpful were *The Gift of Fear*, by Gavin de Becker, and *On Killing*, by Lt. Col. Dave Grossman. These books broadened my understanding of the complexities of war, abuse, and atrocities from the perspective of both survivors and perpetrators. Survivors and perpetrators are at the extremes, but both experience trauma. The effects of war leave its scars on them, and on the millions of survivors and perpetrators worldwide.

The Holy Spirit challenged me to develop a training and healing group with both former perpetrators and survivors of war as participants. It is not a conventional practice, but I knew God led me to design the workshop in this way. I did not know God's purpose, but I was confident the structure was His idea to further His kingdom.

Organizing this group was not only challenging, but a personal struggle for me. I avoided working with perpetrators because of my own childhood victimization, concerned my past might haunt me as I moved into unknown territory. I was saved and healed, but I needed to read Joshua's autobiography before bringing the two groups together. Years earlier, the thought of torture terrified me; now I feared painful memories might be triggered as I entered the mind and behavior of a prior perpetrator.

What might I face physically, mentally, emotionally, socially, and spiritually by reading this book? I needed to "relive" the nightmares again to know I was ready for this shift in ministry from working with survivors to also serving perpetrators. I spent years healing from these episodes, but I had doubts I would make it through the book without a digression into my painful past. Fear brings torment. To remain healthy, I needed to pray.

I chose to believe that I could take this journey and keep solid footing, remaining firmly rooted in my present mental health and spiritual strength. Nevertheless, I did not realize that working with Joshua would force me to confront some of the most destabilizing events from my past.

The most dangerous of these events was the trauma of November 4th, 1990. I was returning to Texas after accepting a consultant position at a psychiatric facility in California, which would require regular trips back and forth from Texas. It was a long but peaceful drive under a full and beautiful harvest moon. Thoughts of God and memories of serene church services warmed my soul. *Perhaps I should go back to church*, I mused. I stopped for fuel in San Antonio at about 11:30 p.m., just four or five hours before I would reach my house. Driving off, I noticed a pickup truck not far behind me. The truck lights blinded me, so after about fifteen minutes, I pulled onto the shoulder to let the truck pass.

It stopped behind me rather than passing. Stunned and suspicious, I pulled back onto the road and adjusted my mirror so the lights were not in my eyes. I kept looking back to see if the truck continued to follow me. I was not afraid—just wary. Were these some young boys out for a joyride? Did someone think I was having car trouble? I was not sure, but I did not want to take any chances.

The truck stayed behind me at a distance. I knew I could not make it all the way home without a fuel stop, and even if I could, I lived on a quiet residential street. Since it was now 2:00 a.m. and I had two more hours to drive, no one would be outside when I arrived, and we did not have cell phones then.

I didn't remember any fuel stations along that route and became a bit concerned. But suddenly, a fuel station appeared on the right, and to my relief it was open. It must have been built sometime after I traveled this road in the past. I exited quickly, but to my horror, the truck pulled off too. As I fueled the car, he parked under some trees about twenty feet away, with the engine still running.

The driver was a middle-aged man, and a woman sat on the passenger seat holding a toddler on her lap. All three of them looked at me with piercing eyes. The small truck sat quietly in the dark, not pulling up for fuel. Alarmed, I hurried inside. The attendant gave me the phone, and I quickly called the police. The truck sped away while I talked with a state trooper.

The trooper asked if I was alone. "Yes," I replied.

With concern and control in his voice, he said, "Then their intent was to harm you. Stay there and we will escort you to the next county. Call your family and let them know you are coming, and what happened." The troopers soon arrived, and they told me there had been incidents of young women being abducted, perhaps by followers of Santeria for sacrifice. I got back in my car, and the officers escorted me to the next county. I had hoped they would escort me all the way home, but to my disappointment, they did not. I was unusually calm, though on alert. *Were those people followers of Santeria? Were they really coming after me?*

I learned later that Santeria is a mixture of Catholicism, Spiritism, and Yoruba and has followers in Mexico and areas along the southern US border. The thought of near capture terrified me, but in survivor fashion, I pressed forward. I paid no attention to the characteristic symptoms of trauma increasing by the day.

Several months passed, filled with crisis after crisis. Someone hijacked and vandalized my car; a dog in my care disappeared; I slipped at work and suffered a nasty ankle sprain. The cast made little difference in the pain level and caused increased stress as I drove the two-hour local commute to work. Cortisone injections, prescribed to decrease ankle pain, had little effect and increased my depression.

Each day seemed an eternity, and every agonizing step endless. I hardly slept, jolting up in bed with every noise. Many nights I sat up, longing for the hours to pass. Body and soul screamed from the overwhelming, relentless assault, and the decision to work 1,500 miles away from my family left me frustrated and lonely. Desperation and despair surrounded me like shadows with their own life force. On the edge, I forced myself to continue. After all, giving up is not an option.

On May 31, 1991, my mind wandered from the psychiatric charts piled in front of me. *Why am I here? Not why am I here at the hospital, but why I am alive? Don't tell me it's for the greater cosmos. There must be more to life than one meaningless struggle after another.*

I took a break and drove to my appointment for ankle rehabilitation, and the chiropractor remarked my body resembled that of a 90-year-old woman. *Yes*, I thought, *stress kills*. Physical therapy provided minimal but critical relief from unrelenting pain.

I hobbled to my car for the uncomfortable return trip to the hospital, convinced that if I hurried, I could finish chart reviews and stay home the next day. I expected heavy traffic, typical for a California freeway during rush hour. I turned the radio on and prepared to spend some hours inching my way down the congested road.

Without warning, a fast-moving vehicle rammed into the back of my car. I heard metal crushing metal. My body jerked, propelling me forward, though I wore my seatbelt. The collision whipped my neck back and forth, and dread filled my soul. I had experienced several accidents over the years, and my body cringed with potential implications. The physical and emotional impact invaded as a persistent, unwelcome and uninvited intruder. *Oh no!* I thought. *Here I go again. I really don't know if I can take any more.* I feared pain and injury would change my world.

The woman who hit my car, the policeman, and even the insurance carrier representative suggested I overreacted. The accident seemed minor from their perspective. But they didn't have my life experience. They hadn't endured numerous car accidents. They didn't lose a dog, have their car stolen, suffer a work accident, and surely, they had different childhood experiences. *If only people understood. If only people cared. How do I survive another day?*

Somehow, I managed to get home. This time, unlike with every other trauma, I could not press on. Physical exhaustion and mental and emotional strain paralyzed me. Assaulted by the accident, my protective shell began to crumble. I resigned my position and returned to Texas. My thoughts unraveled as pieces of childhood experiences intruded without mercy. I whined and whimpered like a child and was unable to manage my emotions. *What will happen to me now? What about Jeff? Will I recover this time?* Overloaded and with no resources left, friends recommended I go to the hospital to rest. At the end of June 1991, I agreed to see a psychiatrist. I was too weak to argue.

During the assessment, the psychiatrist asked endless questions about my present and my past. To my surprise, the psychiatrist asked about sexual assault. I never thought much about this before, and the topic wasn't taught in any of my nursing or psychology courses during the 70s and 80s. I thought all women experienced what I did, so why dwell on it? I was a survivor. Nothing stopped me. I denied the influence of the abuse on my life. The psychiatrist said, "It must be dealt with some time." I reluctantly agreed to hospital admission a week after my accident.

I was unprepared for hospitalization. Rather than the opportunity to rest, I was admitted to a busy psychiatric unit. Physical pain consumed me, and a deluge of medical tests, medication adjustments, cervical traction, physical therapy, ice, and a neck brace invaded my fragile world. During a massage session, I remembered the night I had been stalked. I imagined being captured and controlled by countless people and I asked the therapist, "How would I survive if I was tortured?"

She replied, "I think you only manage with God's grace." I did not quite understand this but hoped one day I might.

The lid was removed—sadness, anger, fear, helplessness, rejection, inadequacy, loneliness, and frustration surfaced. I thought of myself as a dirty washrag. Depressed, tired, nauseated, and disgusted, I grasped for hope. I grieved the abuse, and I was sad I did not have a "child" hood. Yes, I was a child; but I did not experience life as a child. I labored to prevent or put out fires, always on guard. *Could I face the history I hadn't known I had?* The past I knew was bleak enough.

The hospital was not a safe place; at least not spiritually. Some of the patients were involved in New Age activities and shared them with the rest of us. My thoughts became darker, my emotions even more erratic, and I saw images I had never seen before. The spirits were horrific, and my fear was uncontrollable. Sadly, a therapist told our group of wounded women that if we forgave, we would never heal. I needed to get away and insisted on discharge.

Before I left the hospital, I noticed a church service invitation. The Prayer of St. Francis of Assisi captured my attention.

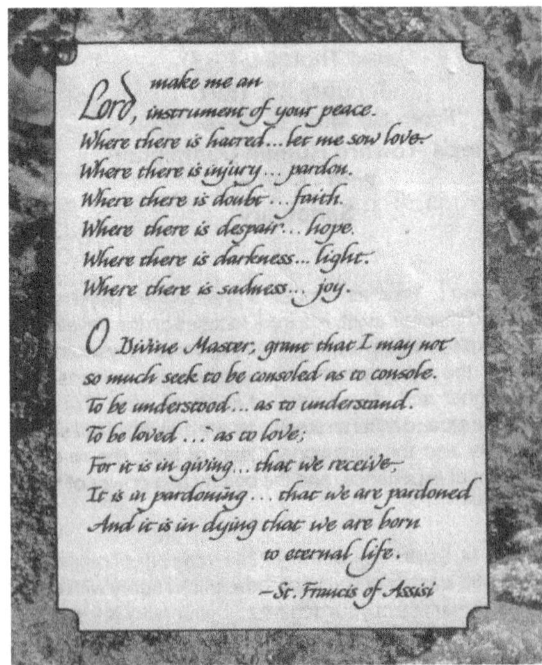

My shaken and hibernating faith stirred. I felt light years away from God. *Was He punishing me? Was He trying to get my attention? Would God help me find my way?*

Though I had forgotten God, He watched over me. I was broken-hearted and crushed in spirit and needed rescue. In my desperation, I cried out to God. His love is relentless and patient, and his salvation is sure. "The Lord looks down from heaven on all mankind to see if there are any who understand, any who seek God" (Psalm 14:2).

After discharge, my family went to Lakewood Church, and Jeff and I went forward for salvation. I'd walked the road before and at times had experiences of deep connection with God. This time I chose to believe and follow—no matter what I felt. If I did not, I would die. Jeff and I were baptized the following week.

Jeremiah 29:11 reads, "'For I know the plans I have for you,' declares the Lord, 'plans to prosper you and not to harm you, plans to give you hope and a future.'" I knew the Scripture in Jeremiah gave promise of hope and a future, but the nation of Israel would go into captivity before the promise would be fulfilled. I too endured captivity until I could rest in the freedom of Christ.

One terrifying night I frantically turned pages in my Bible. There, I read, "Do not be afraid; you will not be put to shame. Do not fear disgrace; you will not be humiliated" (Isaiah 54:4). Though God hid His face from me for a moment, He would have everlasting kindness and mercy for me. He would teach my children and great would be their peace.

Going to church and reading Scripture awakened memories long gone. The hymns and Bible stories truly were old friends who saw me through my troubled youth and now surfaced with refreshing clarity. Bible characters came to life; I saw myself in the pages.

I learned about women of the Bible who had devastating histories, like Rahab, the prostitute who, by her faith and courage, protected the Israelite spies in Jericho. She married one of the spies, and Jesus' bloodline flows through her. Mary Magdalene followed Jesus to the cross after He had cast seven demons from her. And the woman at the well, married five times, became an evangelist after an encounter with Jesus. All of them sinners, saved by grace. All of them are honored in Scripture for their faith. All of them, like the woman who washed the feet of Jesus with her hair, loved much because they were forgiven much. These women gave me hope for life-giving purpose.

It is painful to look back on the darkest part of my life. Memories and years intermingle, and some remain buried in my subconscious. I may never know the entire story since the sexual assault started as a toddler. But my Heavenly Father knows. I give Him permission to share, or not to share, the details of my life. Some are better left in the shadows.

Traumatic experiences took me down a dark path of fear, anxiety, and depression, which took three hospitalizations, many medications—and many years to find healing and recovery. In some ways, the potential kidnapping triggered the question on May 31st, 1991, that ultimately brought me back to faith. *Why am I here?*

Psalm 34:17-18 says, "The righteous cry out, and the Lord hears them; he delivers them from all their troubles. The Lord is close to the brokenhearted and saves those who are crushed in spirit."

Each destructive choice led me closer to death. Unharnessed desires and unhealthy needs lured me toward a bitter end. Proverbs 5:21-23, says. "For your ways are in full view of the Lord, and he examines all your paths. The evil deeds of the wicked ensnare them; the cords of their sins hold them fast. For lack of discipline they will die, led astray by their own great folly." With so little Bible knowledge, I had few resources with which to prevail. A fool does not know she is a fool.

The behavior of others affected me, but I was responsible for my choices. Not others. Not God. Doubt, fear, or sin opens a door for demonic forces to destroy. Proverbs 26:2 reads, "Like a fluttering sparrow or a darting swallow, an undeserved curse does not come to rest." Wounds of the soul open the door for wounds of the spirit. Faulty thoughts, feelings or behaviors destroy life and relationship. Lack of faith, fear, anger, bitterness, revenge, and unforgiveness make us vulnerable. My poor choices opened the door to demonic interference. Patterns emerge and can repeat over generations.

The enemy of my soul and spirit is determined to destroy me and every single person God created. That is his priority and singular mission. Scripture warns us about this evil in I Peter 5:8: "Be alert and of sober mind. Your enemy the devil prowls around like a roaring lion looking for someone to devour."

Yet my misguided choices and the traumatic life-threatening events led to my panic- stricken run to Jesus, from which I have never looked back.

> He reached down from on high and took hold of me; he drew me out of deep waters. He rescued me from my powerful enemy, from my foes, who were too strong for me. They confronted me in the day of my disaster, but the Lord was my support. He brought me out into a spacious place; he rescued me because he delighted in me. (Psalm 18:16–19)

A battle raged for my life. God vs. Satan. When I ran to church, I took a step of faith and dared to believe God overpowers Satan. God laughs at the pride of Leviathan, but not at his deeds. With a clean heart, I could help others avoid the pitfalls that nearly destroyed me. I could trample on fear instead of fear trampling on me.

Chapter Thirteen

The Reconciliation Group

It took some days to process my personal story and its resultant thoughts and feelings. I survived decades of suffering but am grateful for more than thirty years of faith, kindled by the prayer of St. Francis. I would not only "relive" the bitter, but I would "relive" the sweet. It is the brokenness, the sin, that precedes redemption. Jesus, my redeemer, would walk the journey with me. After prayer and self-reflection, I believed I was ready to learn the story of Joshua's past.

Reading Joshua's book caused less internal struggle than I feared, and knowing his history gave me insight into the path he took. His autobiography told the history of the Krahn tribe. It also included Joshua's upbringing and secret initiation as the High Priest at eleven years of age, being advisor to the president of Liberia, and sacrificing children monthly to his god, Nya-bwe-a-weh. The journey gave me a greater understanding of the circumstances leading to his life of atrocity. Exploited as a child, groomed from birth to represent his tribe as the spiritual leader, he knew nothing else. Now a Christian, Joshua relentlessly asks forgiveness for his actions and strives to restore Liberia and to foster peace.

Though I grieved for the trauma Joshua had inflicted, I also grieved for the trauma he experienced as a young boy. And I empathized, knowing he grieves daily as he faces prior survivors and the family members of his victims. He cannot forget how he lived his life, though he knows God forgave him, just as I cannot forget how I lived mine. It took (and continues to take) years for me to experience complete freedom from remnants of darkness deposited in my life. Philippians 1:3-6 reads, "I thank my God every time I remember you. In all my prayers for all of you, I always pray with joy because of your partnership in the gospel from the first day until now, being confident of this, that he who began a good work in you will carry it on to completion until the day of Christ Jesus."

While spiritual salvation is immediate and we are new creations in Christ, healing of the soul is a process. Wounds go deep and change over time, but time alone does not heal. Many people avoid the deep and painful process that typically accompanies healing and transformation. By comparison, the trauma I experienced through violence and dabbling in spirits other than Jesus seems mild compared to Joshua's story. Yet it wasn't negligible.

Romans 3:25-26 reads, "God presented Christ as a sacrifice of atonement, through the shedding of his blood—to be received by faith. He did this to demonstrate his righteousness, because in his forbearance he had left the sins committed beforehand unpunished—he did it to demonstrate his righteousness at the present time, so as to be just and the one who justifies those who have faith in Jesus."

Both Joshua and I suffered terribly because of sins perpetrated against us, and from our own disastrous choices. Though the circumstances were different, much of our journeys were the same. When I came to the end of myself, I ran to church and never looked back. When Joshua encountered the one true God, he dropped his weapons of destruction and picked up a megaphone proclaiming Jesus reigns. After total surrender, we both submitted to a deliverance process to dispel darkness and reflect light. "The path of the righteous is like the morning sun, shining ever brighter till the first light of day" (Proverbs 4:18).

While I ran from fear to the arms of the protector, Joshua sought power from the most powerful God. God knew our motivations and provided what we most desperately needed. Over time, we both had no doubt that the kingdom of darkness is powerless when confronted by the kingdom of Light. Jesus, the King of Kings, reigns forever. His kingdom has no end.

With my soul at rest and confidence restored, the mental health team commenced the reconciliation group. The first day was complicated and intense. I watched for verbal and non-verbal exchanges, keenly aware of everyone entering. I was vigilant, specifically watching two men who asked to participate in the training to receive a greater level of healing: Joshua, a former perpetrator, and Jomah, a survivor of the war.

Jomah's story was opposite Joshua's story in several ways. Before the war, Jomah was a happily married pastor with a passion to lead people to Jesus. During the war, he was shot by rebels and barely escaped with his life. Hospital staff denied Jomah treatment because he was from a different tribe. Jomah's wife worked long hours to keep Jomah in the hospital and to provide him with food, even though he would not receive care. Jomah's arm became infected, and a compassionate health care worker amputated it, thus saving his life. Jomah vowed never to forgive the rebel who shot him or the health care workers who ignored his plea for help.

A few months later, Jomah came face to face with the rebel who had shot him. The rebel's faction was no longer in control, and Jomah could have reported him. Confronted with his enemy, Jomah had a choice. Would Jomah get revenge and turn the man over to the ruling faction, or would he have mercy even though he received none? Bitterness dissolved, and he chose to forgive the rebel, who then became a pastor like Jomah. He also forgave the health care workers, and he and his family opened a medical clinic. He later became a spokesperson for the government ministry supporting people with disabilities. Jomah never lost his passion to share Jesus and partnered with many organizations to show the Jesus film (an evangelistic movie) throughout the country.

On the first day of the workshop, Joshua and his team were seated in the first row when Jomah arrived. Before entering, Jomah paused in the doorway. Joshua looked at Jomah; Jomah looked at Joshua. Neither of them said a word. It would take time for healing to occur among the participants. It was my responsibility to keep the group moving, while not overlooking what each group member experienced during the process.

Joshua shared the story of sacrificing a 3-year-old girl to gain spiritual power for him and for his soldiers. Thousands from the Krahn tribe died while they were under siege in the barracks, so members of the tribe saw Joshua as both a leader and a hero. In the Krahn tribe, human sacrifice is the pathway for power. One mother begged Joshua to sacrifice her daughter, since there were few children left, and the tribe needed power for battle. Joshua refused at first, but the mother insisted. With a heavy heart, Joshua offered this child as a lamb to the slaughter.

He sat motionless after sharing his story. The room was hushed. "But why did God let me do it? Why didn't God protect her? I didn't want to do it ..." Joshua asked, agony in his voice.

I said to Joshua, "God gives us choice. The choices we make cause pain for others and for us. We live with our choices for the rest of our lives." I discussed the book, *God at War*, and how both the spiritual realm and people can make choices that break the heart of God.

Joshua understood and nodded in agreement. He told us that when he became a Christian, he asked God why He had let him sacrifice the child. The Holy Spirit said to him, "Are you, my judge? You have a will."

Joshua sat alone at his desk during the break. Captured by thoughts and memories of his complicated story, he disappeared into a private world of pain. He never had the opportunity to process it with a mental health professional, even though he had been through much deliverance with pastors. I asked Joshua if he wanted to meet with me, apart from attending the group. He said, "Yes. I would."

I met with Joshua weekly to foster God's healing process in his life and trusted God to give me wisdom and insight to see Joshua through this new level of healing. I listened to the Holy Spirit, trusting Him to guide me as I heard Joshua's story. Joshua and I spent hours together, processing his early life—his role as Spiritual High Priest, his transition into the role of a warrior at the death of his President, and his life during and after the war. I knew many details before we began counseling since it was a widely publicized war. I did not know the personal pain of this little boy-man. Driven to darkness from birth, he never experienced life as a child. It crushed him to face his sin. Downcast and despondent, he said, "I know God's grace saved me." He knew God's grace could "save" anyone. He did not know God loved him.

The reconciliation group deepened my relationship with participants as I learned stories from both perpetrators and survivors. I asked Joshua and Jomah to come to "Winds of Hope" to discuss the reconciliation process—how forgiveness opens the door for reconciliation for both survivors and perpetrators. I met with Joshua beforehand and said, "Joshua, you continually confess your crimes and ask for forgiveness. Today I want you to share your personal most painful experience."

Joshua hung his head and nodded. "Yes."

When I asked this question on the radio, he answered, "Actually, my whole life has been pain." We heard the depth of agony he, too, suffered through exploitation and rejection much of his life.

When the group ended, Joshua and Jomah united and traveled around the city bringing a message of repentance, forgiveness, and hope. Together they shared the Jesus film, Jomah beaming, and Joshua sharing his salvation story.

With Joshua, Jomah, and Naomi

As I spend time with Joshua, I see deeper levels of healing in his life. Our capacity to impact others for good increases when we experience the love and grace extended to us. This incredible grace, this unconditional love, seals me and seals Joshua, to the One who loved us before the foundations of the world.

God's light shines brightest in the greatest darkness. God saves to the uttermost, and love covers a multitude of sins. God's light, not my light, shines in the darkness. Joshua's life was touched by this light, and so was mine.

Journal entry, November 2008

> I am amazed at the healing you are doing in my life, Lord. Having been a survivor, I never expected you to position me to work with perpetrators. Yet, you have done it. And to my surprise, you were bringing as much healing for me as for them. Why am I surprised? That's just who you are … the multi-faceted, completely loving Redeemer. Your touch reaches in a thousand directions. Thank you for continuing to deliver me from prejudices and bondage and giving me insight into the blindness and bondage of others.

I took a risk walking into the perpetrator's world. It might lead to memories too strong for me to face. Yet, how do we know we've grown unless we venture forth, confronting the past and entering the future? Would I recoil in horror, or would I step out of my comfort zone into the world of the unknown?

Spiritual enemies storm the mind. They steal our peace. Yet their power pales compared to Jesus. God glorifies Himself, increases our understanding of who He is, gives us greater personal freedom and more territory to set others free. If I don't grow, if I don't share, I can't help others find freedom.

> LORD, you establish peace for us; all that we have accomplished you have done for us. LORD our God, other lords besides you have ruled over us, but your name alone do we honor. They are now dead, they live no more, their spirits do not rise. You punished them and brought them to ruin; you wiped out all memory of them. You have enlarged the nation, LORD; you have enlarged the nation. You have gained glory for yourself; you have extended all the borders of the land. (Isaiah 26:12-15)

Responsibility follows an increase in territory. For this season, I needed to step out further, without conditions. Salvation and grace are not available based on goodness. Jesus took every sin and sickness to the cross. Jude admonishes us:

> But you, dear friends, by building yourselves up in your most holy faith and praying in the Holy Spirit, keep yourselves in God's love as you wait for the mercy of our LORD Jesus Christ to bring you to eternal life. Be merciful to those who doubt; save others by snatching them from the fire; to others show mercy, mixed with fear – hating even the clothing stained by corrupted flesh. (Jude 20–23)

Since my sins are forgiven, and I experience greater freedom through the reconciliation group, I now have increased responsibility to help others find freedom.

Isaiah 61:1-4 reads:

> The Spirit of the Sovereign LORD is on me, because the LORD has anointed me to proclaim good news to the poor. He has sent me to bind up the brokenhearted, to proclaim freedom for the captives and release from darkness for the prisoners, to proclaim the year of the LORD's favor and the day of vengeance of our God, to comfort all who mourn, and provide for those who grieve in Zion—to bestow on them a crown of beauty instead of ashes, the oil of joy instead of mourning, and a garment of praise instead

> of a spirit of despair. They will be called oaks of righteousness, a planting of the Lord for the display of his splendor. They will rebuild the ancient ruins and restore the places long devastated; they will renew the ruined cities that have been devastated for generations. (Isaiah 61:1-4)

Deliverance means more of God and less of evil. We gain confidence each time we take a step of faith and confront our spiritual enemies. Spiritual power increases when we combine confidence in Jesus with submission and obedience. Generations of demonic power, lies, and strongholds crumble to dust.

Chapter Fourteen

Francophone Immersion

The Mental Health Program continued to expand, and with its growth came new challenges amid amazing opportunities. Sailing to various ports, training new provider groups, increasing the number and frequency of interpreters and returning to previous countries to provide follow-up kept the team moving. Lives changed, including ours, and wonderful memories were made.

I returned to the *Africa Mercy* in January 2009. Technical staff prepared the ship for sail and for ten months on location, while program staff prepared for field service projects. Surgeries and other life-giving services exist not only because of health care professionals but also the technical crew and volunteers who serve in hospitality, the galley, the dining room, the bank, reception, and the Academy. It takes a village to raise a child. It takes a multinational and multi-talented group of like-minded people to provide holistic care through Mercy Ships. Donations, including coffee, revitalize the crew when they need a lift through physical, psychological, social or spiritual care. Crew gather in the lounge to share their hopes, successes, struggles and to build relationships which last for weeks or a lifetime.

The *Africa Mercy* was on the move, and we sailed from the Canary Islands through choppy waters with a dreary grey sky overhead. But the weather changes quickly at sea. We entered calm seas and sunned ourselves under a strikingly beautiful blue sky. Crew lined the decks, as dolphins entertained us in the water below. These magnificent creatures danced with elegance and poise—perhaps they knew we admired them.

We arrived in Benin, a Francophone (French-speaking) country in West Africa. Benin is considered the cradle of Voodoo and is deeply entrenched in witchcraft. People from all over the globe attend the Voodoo festival held on January 10th each year.

> Journal entry, February 21, 2009
>
> Over 2,500 people sought care during screening this week. It's painful to watch them struggle with life-altering deformities and life-threatening conditions. Some of the people are carried because they can't walk and don't have a wheelchair. Little children lead their blind parents. I remember the string of blind people, holding on to each other in Liberia.
>
> Can we be kind enough? Will their wounds heal? You know, Lord. You know. The crew on a Mercy Ship bring hope and healing to a sea of people through physical, emotional and spiritual care. In most cases, joy dispels despair, and seeds of hope are planted.

My responsibility, however, was to continue development of and implement the mental health program, and to integrate global strategies for mental health care. The World Health Organization developed the Optimal Mix of Mental Health Services with the goal to increase mental health services in areas of low capacity, and gear the process toward self-care, informal care, and primary health care to decrease strain on mental health professionals.

The Mercy Ships mental health team had already put that approach into practice, but I was keenly aware the Holy Spirit was responsible for alignment with global strategy. God opened doors for various provider groups. The only part I contributed was asking for church leaders to be included in training, and I have no doubt God inspired that vision as well. He knows the end from the beginning.

It became clear that ordination increased credibility. Both in Liberia and in Benin, high-level church leaders attended training. Skepticism of mental health and psychology is the norm, so integrating a spiritual perspective increases acceptance. Being ordained as a chaplain was a preference, but for serving global church leaders—it was critical. When I or any of my team members say we are ordained, participants relax and engage with curiosity for what lies ahead.

Settled in Benin, the mental health team joined with leaders to organize the upcoming workshop. Few of the leaders spoke English, and none of us spoke French, which complicated implementation. I worked with interpreters in the past, but not for full weeks of training. My team members listened intently as the interpreter and I communicated to sort out details. Somehow, I made it through the planning session, and the organizers understood what we were saying. I relaxed.

Communication, however, also occurs through body language. A smile to build connection; a hug (when appropriate and welcomed); proximity; head nodding when there are no words. I took two years of French in high school, and two years of Spanish at university. And I lived in Germany for four years in a rural village. While I do not have a gift of language, my few words often bridge the gap with guidance from the Holy Spirit when interpreters aren't available. One of the greater difficulties is sharing mealtimes with participants. To have a meaningful conversation, it requires one of our interpreters to spend their break time working. Language barriers are some of the most difficult areas for me to overcome in serving the nations. I often isolate, and some may think it's by choice. Others may think I don't want to build relationships.

Mealtimes, however, are opportunities to model Jesus. Our team, when possible, assists with serving, removing dirty dishes and picking up trash. This is often foreign to the participants. One day I had finished my meal and asked a prominent church leader if I could carry his plate to the caterers. He looked shocked. "You would carry my plate?" he said.

I replied, "Surely. I'm finished with my meal and carrying mine."

"We have so much to learn," He responded.

It is my desire to be downwardly mobile, like Jesus, and a model of servanthood.

One of the more uncomfortable situations I face is leaders inviting me for a meal in their homes. Often, the wife prepares the food for the men, and of course for me. The women then eat in the kitchen. This is a cultural preference and not a principle, but it is difficult for me to be included with the men because of my position when the other women are eating in another room with the children. It does not happen in all cultures, and it is not my place to change it. But I do my best to include women and children whenever possible.

Benin differed significantly from Liberia. Liberia is a country primarily settled by freed American slaves, so Liberians have adopted many American customs in addition to the language. Ancestors of most Liberians, and thousands of people today, have lived in

America, so I am more at home in Liberia than in any other African country. Most Liberians have a tribal name but also an American name, and though they speak "Liberian English," with careful listening I understand the general meaning. Benin was colonized by the French, so its culture is a deep mixture of French with centuries of tribal practices. French influence continues to dominate Benin and most other Francophone countries in Africa.

The mental health workshop commenced with high-level church leaders and government officials. Koumabe, a minister and educator, told a story of a man who had headaches and exhibited bizarre behavior. The church leaders cast out demons, but the man did not improve. One leader had said, "We should send him to the hospital," and on examination, the man was found to have a terminal brain tumor. Koumabe purposed to use the information he learned at the workshop by studying other areas of the whole person to identify where problems originate. He learned to see things through not only a spiritual lens. He remarked that he studied theory at university but learned how to apply it during the mental health training workshop. Koumabe became a member of the mental health team, and his family and I developed a deep friendship. He continues to foster mental health treatment and is a professor at the University.

Soon after, I met with the national mental health coordinator for Benin, a well-known and respected psychiatrist who incorporated traditional healing into his practice. Leaders of other faith groups are often skeptical of partnering together, concerned our team will impose Christianity on participants. He asked me a question from a traditional perspective and waited for my response. "Do you believe if a man is in emotional pain and holds the blanket his mother gave him to his heart his mother will feel his pain?"

I said, "I believe a mother's love reaches through time and space by the Spirit."

Content with my response, the professor asked for training in Abomey, since he planned to retire and build a center based on traditional practices. I strive to find similarities between faith groups and develop bridges to break down dividing walls.

Abomey was a three-hour drive from the ship, so it required creative thinking. A former Mercy Ships colleague had a self-sustaining children's home nestled in Abomey. We made this my base and invited department heads from the *Africa Mercy* to join me each week. They provided specific aspects of expertise and gained first-hand exposure to the mental health training.

My friend gave the children under her care a home for the rest of their lives. I developed great relationships with the children through the weekly visits and by offering a children's trauma healing workshop. The children learned coping skills to help them now and for the future and received healing from past wounds. One girl, about twelve years old, drew my attention as she seemed isolated and paralyzed, unable to build relationships with other children. Over time, this child learned social skills, developed coping skills to counter her own negative thoughts, and made friendships.

Every day was filled with new experiences. I learned how to play the djembe drum (poorly), and how to paint white fingernail polish on dark-colored fingernails. At 5:00 a.m. I heard the children and workers worshipping and respected their commitment. And I even learned a bit of tribal language. I could say *tree*, *I'm tired*, and *I'm not tired*. I even learned the French song the children sing to "yovos" (white people), and I would smile and sing along with them: "Yovo, Yovo, bonsoir. Ça va bien, merci!"

Serving among multiple nations, languages, cultures, and faith groups is riddled with complexities, which requires flexibility, courage, and humility. It behooves me to remain vigilant, to adapt to the environment without forgetting who I am and who I represent. I desire to share truth with love. Spending time with Jesus assures the anchor holds.

Meanwhile, in Liberia, results from the Truth and Reconciliation Commission were released, and there was an attempt on Joshua's life following the recommendation for amnesty. The news triggered a night of terror for me as I considered his near-death experience amid the dark forces surrounding me in Abomey. Death is often unpredictable.

Journal entry, July 31

> Do we look to others for approval or direction on who we should be? We teach the children in the workshop they are special—no two flowers are alike—no two people are the same. Can we allow God to mold us, not as lifeless clay but as vibrant and fragrant bouquets created by Him—for His pleasure and ours? Are we growing into our God-given purpose, whether it fits with what others want us to do? Do we have the courage to trust God to lead us where He wants us, even if it means letting go of what is familiar? I understand I must lose my life—I am not sure how it will look or what will happen—but I know that by dying I will surely live. By losing my life I will surely find it. Take me deeper into self-sacrifice, to gain greater peace as my soul rests in You.

A brief return to the US provided space and time for spiritual renewal and reflection, which prepared me for Haiti, another nation influenced by France and steeped in witchcraft. Haiti literally crumbled after an enormous earthquake. My role was to debrief staff who worked at the mission compound. I heard heart-wrenching stories of their earthquake experience, and their selfless acts of love. Debriefing gave an opportunity for workers to understand their team member's unique earthquake experiences.

SIL and Wycliffe developed a helpful model in which the grief process is described as movement through three villages. This model is a simple yet effective way to visualize walking through grief. I have changed the name of the second village in the model from the Village of No Hope to the Valley of Weeping, and I use this revised model in all the training or healing workshops.

After a short session on the five models and the grief process, I focused on the Behavior Process Model by asking the following questions: "What happened? What did you think? What did you feel, physically and emotionally? What did you do? What helps you cope?" As I asked these questions, survivors quietly shared their stories. No two stories were alike, and each person processed the situation in a different way. One kitchen worker described watching her 4-year-old son die in front of her.

Her supervisor looked at me and said in a hushed voice, "I didn't know."

The mother said, "Everyone is suffering. I didn't want to put more pressure on them."

This mother coped through silence and concern for others.

The room was silent; partly because team members experienced guilt for not having asked each other about their experiences, and partly because they vividly remembered their own crises during the earthquake. This time of group debriefing provided a physical and emotional space for survivors to hear each other's stories and find ways to support their coworkers going forward. In telling stories, people connect. A listening ear. A gentle touch. Shared tears. Without such an encounter, people are tempted to move quickly into new beginnings, choosing to jump over the pain rather than walk through the villages. Unfortunately, this leads to unhealed trauma. Following the debrief, coworkers received a new level of empathy and relationship with the team because of the shared experience.

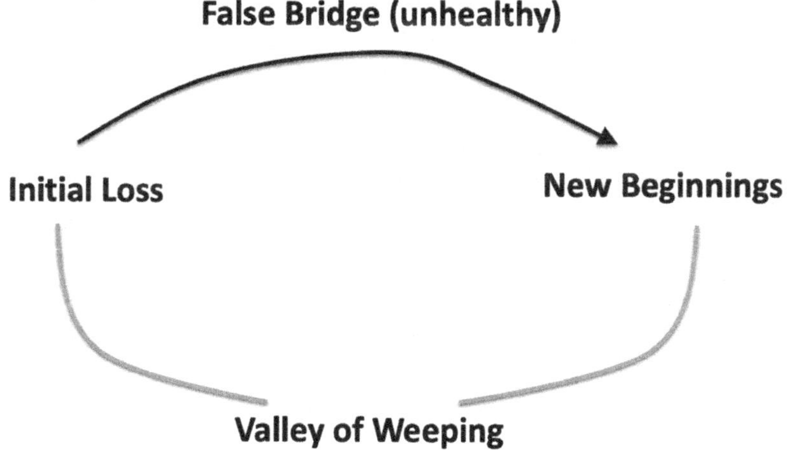

I offered a workshop for teachers to debrief, then mentally and emotionally prepare them for classrooms with empty chairs—some teachers and some children were victims of the tragedy. Some children would return as orphans. When a crisis hits, the world turns upside down. People are destabilized, and in most cases, unable to process what's happening. The training allowed teachers to share their own experiences, and to gain tools to support each other and the children upon return. They, too, would be hearing stories.

Practical support is important, but giving themselves and the children an opportunity to share helps everyone grieve. The teachers learned they might see changes in behavior in the children, and were equipped with new ways to work with them in these circumstances. Most people heal from trauma, but they will never be the same as they were before the traumatic event. It's important for leaders to know this about themselves and those they serve.

Jesus is always with me, and the Holy Spirit leads the way as I navigate languages, cultures, environmental stressors, and tragic stories. I don't need to know the path; I just need to follow the leader.

I thought about a trip I made years earlier between projects with another crew member to Mont-Saint-Michel, a majestic island on the coast of France. The train stopped suddenly, and the conductor motioned for us to leave. We learned that another train had crashed in front of us, and we needed to take a bus. We didn't know the route; we didn't speak French, and the other passengers spoke little English. Voices buzzed as people tried to figure out how to help us.

Darkness fell during our seemingly aimless bus ride. After some hours a young man got up and looked directly at us. "Follow me," he directed. Immediately, we left the bus and followed him. We watched the bus drive off as we stood with the man on the silent and deserted street. How would we get to the hotel up the hill? The man read our hotel address, then used the payphone and called the hotel to send a driver. He managed to lead us to our destination using his limited English.

The spiritual intensity of Benin and Haiti resurfaced my tortuous past following the voice of spirits other than Jesus. Now I followed a man though I couldn't understand his words. I mused, *If I can follow someone I don't know from a bus because I am lost in France, how much more should I follow Jesus, who is, and was, and ever will be?* Our journey pivots when we cross the barrier between the visible and the invisible. Do we trust what we can't see? Will we follow the right voice?

Matthew 4:18-20 (ESV) tells the story of Jesus calling two fishermen, Simon Peter and his brother Andrew, while they were casting their nets into the Sea of Galilee. "And he said to them, 'Follow Me, and I will make you fishers of men.' Immediately they left their nets and followed Him."

Immediately. I, too, will follow where He leads, even if He leads in a direction I do not want to go. Jesus sent me a cooler filled with fish in 1996 before I left for Mercy Ships as confirmation that as I follow Him, I become a fisher of men. Though I may not regularly see people become followers of Jesus, I plant, or water seeds leading people in His direction. God brings the increase.

CHAPTER FIFTEEN

Transitions, Trials, and Tribes

The year 2010 marked a turning point in the mental health program. The *Africa Mercy* planned a short field service in Togo to allow for time in shipyard in Durban, South Africa. Crew beds reached critical capacity, and since the Mental Health Program was implemented off-ship, management decided to use mental health crew beds for hospital staff. The two mental health team members left after the field service ended. However, two Togolese pastors, Samuel and Sóule, joined as local team members and continue to travel with the team internationally.

Missions is intense, as is serving in low-and-middle-income nations. Poverty, civil or international conflicts, disease, and corruption complicate the work. Though environmental variables may create difficulties in any part of the world, these nations face considerably more frequent and more severe obstacles. Our team often faces challenges once we are on the road or during training. Going forward, I needed to learn how to develop, implement, and lead the Mental Health Program with fewer ties to one of the ships. Environmental security issues are paramount, so detached from a ship the team would need to be keenly aware of potential dangers.

For example, an opportunity arose for the team to provide training for teachers, police, military, corrections officers, and magistrates and the workshop was scheduled with the high court as the venue. The ship's chief engineer joined us to discuss how stress affects performance from a technical perspective, but that day training was delayed because of a riot over exorbitant fuel costs and a high-profile court case. We were caught in stalled traffic, and hostile crowds surrounded us.

We radioed the security officer on the *Africa Mercy* and asked whether we should try to get back to the ship or try to move forward to the courthouse. I agreed with the decision to proceed. Better to hold tight in a hurricane's eye than to swirl aimlessly in prevailing winds. We finished training that day but lost six hours. Experiencing and managing real-life stress is a better teacher than "what if" scenarios. This incident occurred with ship security staff giving direction. Day-to-day resources would look different as the Mental Health Program moved forward independently of the ship.

The *Africa Mercy's* field service was complete, and preparations began for shipyard. The ship set sail, and I volunteered for another one of my favorite jobs—pirate watch. I loved standing on the bow with one of our Nepali Gurkhas, watching for pirates, listening to the waves, and dreaming of South Africa. The elite Gurkha fighting force had famously prevented the British from colonizing Nepal. Eventually, the British signed a treaty and hired them, impressed with their unique skill. Mercy Ships hires trained Gurkhas to provide security for the crew and ship, and we are privileged to have them. I am privileged to call them friends.

To many, standing pirate watch sounds like fun. But pirates are not Captain Hook, standing on the bow of a wooden boat with his spyglass and a motley crew. Today's pirates are sophisticated, employ highly technical navigation and weapons, and would love the opportunity to seize a ship staffed by humanitarian workers from over thirty-five nations. It is not a game, and we take the responsibility seriously.

Being able to sail was a precious gift, since I hadn't been scheduled to sail; there was no funding for an off-ship program in South Africa. But I love to pray, and prayer changes things. God provided funding through the UK Mercy Ships office two weeks before the sail, and the *Africa Mercy* programs administrator worked steadily, quickly and effectively to find local partners. Weekly projects were scheduled across the Zulu nation, and a team member and I formed precious memories.

We stayed in a typical Zulu hut and drove through the Hluhluwe-iMfolozi Park on the Elephant Coast. We marveled at the lush grasslands, expansive rolling hills, and variety of greenery. We saw men and women in clothing splashed with red, green, blue, orange, and yellow. One Zulu chief told my friend he wanted to marry her.

She said, "I am already married."

He said, "I will give you a mansion."

She said, "I already have one."

My friend is married to the King of Kings, who has a mansion waiting for her.

Watching animals energizes me and brings me joy. We prayed to see animals, and animals, including zebras and giraffes, dotted the countryside. Two elephants relaxed, as if posing for a photo. We turned a corner and saw a rhino and then a buffalo, standing lazily in the grasslands. Each day burst with wonder and surprise. The rich experiences of hearing a different language, using local currency, driving on the left side of the road, and living off the ship remain in our hearts and memories. All these experiences better equip me not only to understand the geography, the culture, and some nuances of language and behavior, but also to live on the ground with the people I serve, rather than on a world-class ship. This was an important lesson in how to navigate the future.

One evening, a team member and I had dinner at a local restaurant. We noticed a table of men who kept looking at us while whispering among themselves. I unabashedly asked them what they were talking about.

One man said, "We think you must be married to the same man."

This was not a response either of us expected, so I replied, "Why would you think that?"

The man answered, "You get along so well together."

The next day in training, I shared the experience with the church leader training group and asked, "Is this common? Do you agree with this?" To my surprise, both men and women agreed it is common practice, and that good relationships are maintained among the wives. Open discussions are necessary to better understand cultures and the degree to which they line up with Scripture.

Two experiences stand out because I saw God respond to my prayers in a direct way. The longer we walk with Jesus, the more we know He is our sufficiency. Though we are to be interdependent with people, we are to depend on Him. I shared a drawing I made, showing how Jesus works through the local church to meet the needs of people. I told the church leaders that if they ask God to bring the unloved, the outcasts, the desperate from the community to the church, their churches will grow. And if they go into the communities and connect with people, their churches will grow. I reminded them Jesus looked for the one sheep who strayed rather than staying with the ninety-nine sheep.

Participants were challenged by allowing "unusual" people to come to church, because they might not have a sound mind or acceptable behavior. Church leaders were geared toward feeding the flock they had rather than opening the door for potential chaos. This training was split over a weekend, so participants returned to their local areas for two days. When they came back to training, one pastor said he prayed for God to draw anyone He wanted to the church, and the pastor committed to accept all who would come. Several new people came to church that day, and several who had left the church some time before suddenly returned. His story encouraged other pastors to do the same.

The group completed the workshop, and on the last day of training, I asked participants to write their pain on pieces of paper to give to God. We gathered in a circle around a box placed in the middle to collect the papers. Rain pitter-pattered on the ground, and I couldn't find a dry place to put the box. I am a poor fire-starter, so I said, "I am not Elijah." I lit the match, but the pages did not burn. I then said, "Breath of Heaven, light this fire." God sent fire and consumed not only the papers—their sacrifice—but also the box. What a Holy moment; every person stood silently. The computer image of the photo revealed a cross in the fire.

Thank you, Jesus, for your sacrifice. You consume our pain. And when we depend on You instead of ourselves, we see miracles. It was a lesson both for the participants and for the team. God is determined to see His kingdom come on earth as it is in heaven, and He reminded me that the Mental Health Program matters. His heart breaks over suffering caused by disasters, epidemics and pandemics, technological accidents, and war. It also breaks for the outcast, and for those who live through cultural divides such as apartheid in South Africa.

The South Africa project ended, and I needed to make decisions about the future. Though I learned the Mental Health Program could function outside of the ship structure, it was more complicated. The possibility of the Mental Health Program changing course or even ceasing to exist unnerved me. How would I lead a program while not physically present and with no team members to set up logistics? Settled into my role and ministry, I resisted change.

I then remembered a line from *Braveheart*: "Your heart is free; have the courage to follow it!" The situation and its outcomes lost their grip. I must follow Jesus—no matter what comes and no matter where He leads. I could stay with Mercy Ships, or branch out into other nations, or I could do both. But how?

We all face challenges and are sometimes forced to make decisions we don't want to make. My understanding of cultures, languages, and God's heart for the world grew deeper in each place I served. Sleeping in huts, dancing tribal dances, worshipping in a language foreign to my own, gave me unique moments in time and space. I loved my life, and savored every minute of every day. I believed that God had a plan, and I would soon learn the next steps.

PART FOUR.
LIVING ON THE EDGE

Chapter Sixteen

The Gift of Homelessness

> Journal entry, January 1, 2011
>
> It seems I'm being prepared to sacrifice something. What is it, Lord? I dare to live on the edge, not knowing what lies ahead. Fifteen years ago, I trusted You for a short mission trip. Now I trust You for world-changing opportunities. Guide me as I step out in greater faith, for greater impact.

I wondered if God was leading me to surrender my apartment by the lake, so I decided to prayer walk in the woods. The thought of moving was difficult for me because my work is fast-paced and intense. When I return to my "sanctuary" I take time for physical, mental, emotional, social and spiritual rest. The Holy Spirit said, "Don't you think I can give you something as nice or nicer when the time is right?" Yes, Lord, I know you can. It seemed logical. Spending money on rent made no sense since I worked internationally for months at a time. I put some belongings in storage, gave away others, and loaded my car.

Downsizing was easy, and mobility a breeze. I'd certainly done it many times before. The combination of housing and career instability shook me, but only for a season. I've learned through experience that change is a catalyst for opportunity and for adventure. Jesus led an adventurous life, riddled with instability. Jesus was downwardly mobile. I want to be downwardly mobile, too. Downward mobility coupled with humility ushers in spiritual power.

Rebuilding the Mental Health Program required smart strategies and a newly crafted team. The program was at risk if I failed to build an altered structure. I chose faith and dove headfirst to pilot a unique and sustainable program. Destabilizing challenges loomed ahead as I left the safety of living onboard when offering projects abroad. An enlarged territory may look different from what you expect. Twists and turns are the norm on uncharted waters. But God already knows the path and is the captain of my ship.

The Mental Health Program structure had changed, but the projects remained the same. I learned how to make the program work with floating staff, and without a designated workspace. We planned to offer workshops in multiple locations during 2011 and 2012, and potential projects blossomed in several nations each year going forward. Since I was no longer tied to a forty-hour-plus work week with Mercy Ships, I could partner with other organizations to offer mental health projects. I embraced one of my favorite Scriptures, Isaiah 54:2-3: "Enlarge the place of your tent, stretch your tent curtains wide, do not hold back; lengthen your cords, strengthen your stakes. For you will spread out to the right and to the left; your descendants will dispossess nations and settle in their desolate cities."

Sierra Leone

I made plans to travel back to West Africa in the winter of 2011. I flew to Sierra Leone, then took a twenty-minute speedboat ride to the *Africa Mercy* at 2:00 a.m. I was the only passenger on board, which provided a hiatus from the whirlwind of long-term missions. My soul settled with the cool breeze and the salt-licked air.

This was my first visit since the fall of 2000, and I collaborated with a faith-based organization that had limited resources. Their operations were based in a circa-1500 stone building that housed tormented souls. The air was damp and musty; some levels were near darkness, and lower levels reeked of urine. Treatment consisted of prayer, Scripture, and medications provided by a psychiatrist who made occasional visits. Patients bought their own chains to keep themselves from hurting others or from hurting themselves. They were attached to them physically; emotionally, the chains were their only possessions.

My personal experience of hospitalization, medication, and torment more than thirty years ago triggers huge compassion for people amid such darkness. Though I have come to the other side, I vividly remember the relentless agony. I identify with them and give them hope by communicating that Jesus is the healer and transformation is possible. His healing prescription is unique to each individual, and service providers are wise to follow His lead as we care for those He puts in our path.

The founder and spiritual director suffered much in his own life, and as a result, developed deep faith. He desired to please God and to set captives free. He struggled daily to serve people, even though he had limited finances and no formal education. The founder did the best he could considering he served a marginalized population in a nation devastated by war. A Christian social worker raised funds, recruited workers, provided treatment, and increased awareness about mental health and mental disorders. The combination of psychiatric and spiritual care together brought healing in the lives of many patients who were in treatment at the center.

A friend and colleague, Wayna joined the project in Sierra Leone. I met Wayna in 1992 when I was young in faith, stumbling through life, and desperate for spiritual growth. I trusted her, and she and her children surrounded Jeff and me during some of our most painful times.

Wayna writes:

> All my adult life I wanted to go to Africa, and in His perfect timing the Lord gave me clear direction to go. He miraculously

> provided the funds—as I was a single woman with little to no reserve. But it was clear, and He did it as I stepped into trusting Him. It was incredible. The word He gave me earlier that year for my life was "Believe." I did, and He amazed me. My life has changed, and my faith has grown so much since the trip.
>
> Lyn has learned to trust God completely; she has learned this through testing. I had absolute respect for what He was showing her and how she was able to do so much with such favor. But I had no idea how it would be to follow Lyn around; learn the tools the Lord had given her and watch it unfold from concept to delivery. The responses of the pupils were so beautiful. Just as important, I learned to use the tools myself. My perceptions have shifted. I know God is faithful, but I have now learned to take steps in the healing process. I ask myself questions that shift responsibility to me—not to hold others responsible. And I share these perceptions with those God puts in my path.

Wayna hand-carried five dolls a friend of hers bought from secondhand stores. The friend beautified the throw away dolls, just as Jesus beautifies us when we let Him purchase and clean us up. Our team members now use the dolls to share hope with children who think they have no value. My doll, Benjamin Alexander, is a reminder that I am no longer a throw away doll. Jesus cleaned me up, gave me new clothes, and paid a high price for me.

Togo

The *Africa Mercy* traveled on to Togo and captured follow-up stories from previous participants. A few years earlier, I realized follow-up not only gives me an opportunity to measure progress, but it reminds participants they are valued regardless of their successes. Several participants told me that they know I care because I come back. This is a valuable life lesson. People are not a project or a goal. They are intricately woven into our lives if we let them in.

The mental health team met with the Ministry of Defense, Civil Action, Justice, and Prison Fellowship. A magistrate shared that in the past he determined sentences based solely on facts. Now he employs the Behavior Process Model and listens to the stories to get the defendant's perspective. *Why did the defendant do what he did?*

He told the story of a man from one tribe who kidnapped a woman from another tribe. The offender went to jail defiant and angry, since he didn't understand why he couldn't steal women. The magistrate decided to visit the man in prison. After listening to the offender's story, he said, "I understand that in your tribe it is acceptable to take a woman if you want her. But in the woman's tribe, it is not acceptable. And Togo has laws against what you did. You must respect the rights of others if you want your rights to be respected." The offender then understood and agreed not to take women in the future. As a result, the magistrate lightened his sentence.

I took a side trip to the UK on my return to the US for a break. The Mercy Ships Board met, and I gave an update on the Mental Health Program. In-person communication offers an opportunity for greater understanding of the program's relevance and often increases financial support. Don Stephens asked, "How many people do you think are influenced by the Mental Health Program?" His question has merit and is not rhetorical. *Does what we do make a difference?* Don was not asking to reduce people to numbers but to measure effectiveness and determine if adjustments are necessary.

I answered, "Don, it is not possible to measure the effectiveness of the Mental Health Program in the same way we count surgeries or dental procedures. If one boy learns not to touch girls inappropriately, how many lives does that affect? If church leaders offer counseling or refer people with unusual behavior to medical professionals when appropriate rather than cast out demons, how many people receive healing? If a husband stops beating his wife, what is the impact on the family? We can measure the number of people attending training, but we cannot determine the number of those positively affected. Surely thousands have been impacted."

On November 4th, I made a detour to Bethel Church in California. I hoped to receive a fresh touch from the Holy Spirit. I declared my desperation for Jesus as I knelt during worship and thanked God for his faithfulness. A man from the row behind me leaned over and handed me his prophetic artwork. The picture showed me kneeling with my head down before the Lord; God's hand reached out with a flask, pouring a fresh anointing on my head. A dam broke inside me, feeling a sense of relief because my loving Father heard my heart's cry. I wanted more, so I stayed for prophecy, seeking words of wisdom that might apply specifically to me.

The condensed prophecy:

> I feel like you're a woman who understands classiness well, which you usually don't say to a missionary. I think you understand this in different cultures; I also think you are a woman of God with

> a lot of revelation from the Lord, and you've applied that in wise ways to numerous different kinds of communities throughout the years. You haven't hoarded that up for yourself.
>
> Sometimes the structures that you're in haven't always been conducive to freely dispensing of the revelation, but you stewarded it well. The Lord has seen what you've done with it, and He is pleased. I feel you carry such a sweetness, sweet love of God, and the words you speak are like honey to the soul. The honey is covering them as soon as you start to speak over them. It's healing for them. Maybe you don't even recognize how powerful your words are for them; but God says they are so strong, and they create an amazing atmosphere, a safe place and healing and restoration in the people you are ministering to.
>
> You are a favored daughter, and you can go beyond normal heights. The way He's wired you, you reach those heights without trying to leap because you know who you are in the Lord. God, I pray for more joy, more favor, more blessing than she has ever seen. And for more fruit, God, in what she's doing; more souls, more healing and restoration, everywhere she steps.

The prophecy led to reflection on the past year and the rapidly changing seasons. Choosing to leave my nest left me completely homeless, with only a storage unit. This was the first time in my life I had no home. I loved the apartment by the lake. It was small, but I was settled into my own space, surrounded by beauty. Yet, I knew God remained by my side as I hurled myself into the land of the homeless. After all, I followed His directive. He promised something even better someday.

I was in good company—Jesus was homeless. Luke 9:57-58 reads, "As they were walking along the road, a man said to him, 'I will follow you wherever you go.' Jesus replied, 'Foxes have dens and birds have nests, but the Son of Man has no place to lay his head.'" In contrast to Jesus, I always have somewhere to lay my head. The world is now my home.

Mark 10:29-30: "'Truly, I tell you,' Jesus replied, 'no one who has left home or brothers or sisters or mother or father or children or fields for me and the gospel will fail to receive a hundred times as much in this present age; homes, brothers, sisters, mothers, children and fields—along with persecutions—and in the age to come eternal life.'" God directs my steps, provides for me and arranges houses for me to stay far beyond what I could personally afford. He gives me havens across the United States and, at times, internationally.

We get tired. I get tired. The day at Bethel restored me. Psalm 18:28-33 (ESV) says, "For it is You who light my lamp; the Lord my God lightens my darkness. For by You I can run against a troop, and by my God I can leap over a wall. This God—His way is perfect; the word of the Lord proves true; He is a shield for all those who take refuge in Him. For who is God, but the Lord? And who is a rock, except our God? —the God who equipped me with strength and made my way blameless. He made my feet like the feet of a deer and set me secure on the heights."

> Journal entry, November 4, 2012
>
> November 4, 1990, I was likely stalked by members of Santeria on the terrorizing drive from California to Texas. Here I am, November 4th, 22 years later—still driving between California and Texas, but with a different story. This visit I traveled to California seeking God at Bethel. I am a new person. But Jesus was beside me in 1990 as He's beside me now. 22 years ago—I ran from darkness. Today—I run toward Light. I John 4:4 reads, "You, dear children, are from God and have overcome them, because the one who is in you is greater than the one who is in the world."

I traveled many roads without Jesus and now have traveled many more with Him. I know His plans are purposeful. While I might be shaken, I do not fall. I know Who lives inside me, who gives me life and godliness. Enemies come in many forms, from little foxes to earth-shattering decisions. He has overcome the enemies of my soul. Ultimately, He leads, if I let Him.

The encouragement and inspiration I received through the drawing and the prophecy at Bethel settled my spirit and stirred my passion for my next adventures. The years 2011 and 2012 ended, and a new year peeked over the horizon. No need to fear the future. God walks beside me and knows the plans He has for me.

Chapter Seventeen

Pitch and Roll

I confess—2013 rocked my boat. Trials come in all forms, and during that year I faced both work-related and physical challenges. Clearly, I was unprepared for the upcoming obstacles. Nevertheless, I moved onward; unaware I had entered the gauntlet.

I returned to Sierra Leone to fulfill a request for training from the liaison for traditional healers. This unique group of practitioners is often ostracized, since they have different levels of education and a wide variety of treatment approaches. They traveled from all areas of Sierra Leone and paid their own transportation to receive training.

On the first day, one of the traditional healers arrived with a talisman to protect himself from other spirits. The senior leader told him to remove the talisman; there was no place for items of spiritual power in this group. Most participants had practiced their craft for decades, yet they came with humility and a desire to learn. One seasoned and powerful traditional healer moved close to the flip chart during break to make detailed notes. His eyes were dim, but his heart was huge. He wanted to grasp this different approach to healing, so contrary to his own.

Our team learned much from them as well. Female genital mutilation (FGM) is of concern in many low-and-middle-income nations and continues to be widely practiced in certain geographical areas and in secret societies. Some organizations avoid the topic, not wanting to offend participants. However, the practice is illegal, and the World Health Organization (WHO) promotes curtailing FGM. The mental health training is designed to address controversial topics, but to do so with love and an attempt to seek to understand rather than to be understood.

I presented the topic during the training. During a break several young women were in the room with me, and I asked how many had experienced FGM. All of them said they had. I then asked, "Would you desire to have it done to yourself or your daughters?"

All of them replied, "No." Their heads hung low, and there was a hush in the room. None of us spoke. I could not have discussed their personal experiences in the mixed group of men and women, and it required trust among us for them to be willing to share. They knew I would not judge, and it reinforced how critical it is to take time to build relationship and establish trust to learn the real stories of those around me.

> Journal entry, March 21, 2013
>
> I woke to the sound of drums from the secret society Bindi, which holds a month-long initiation for young girls. So much violence exists in the name of culture. In most training workshops, participants recoil from snakes. The traditional healers had no fear. They use snakes as part of their practice. Help me see behind the natural. I ask for understanding of the power they hold. Please use these hand-selected men and women as change agents for good. I ask for Your power, wisdom and love.

Spending time with Joshua and working alongside traditional healers provided opportunities to work cooperatively, rather than discount anything foreign to Christianity as inherently evil. Witchcraft and sorcery are often weapons of destruction, but what I hoped to discover was the underlying spiritual principles. Did everything associated with traditional healing destroy life and relationship, or did aspects of these practices foster healthy life and relationship? Eternal issues aside, how might I build bridges to work collaboratively with those of other faith groups, and build relationships to share biblical truths?

The 1998 *Time* magazine article I read while waiting to take the psychologist licensing exam began to make sense. Felfiel, aged 13, had been forced into combat and fought for the government side of the war against family and neighbors. Eventually, Felfiel escaped and walked for three days to return to his village. The villagers allowed him to go through the forgiving rites of traditional cleansing. Felfiel's mother sent him to the spiritual guardian to obtain a *muti*, a substance that brings physical and psychological cleansing. After three days, Felfiel stopped vomiting up the "bad things" he had done. He had earned atonement. Felfiel stopped having nightmares, and the villagers received him back again. The article stated: "Call it witchcraft if you like, but such rural healing is a major reason that nearly 95,000 demobilized soldiers and five million refugees have been absorbed back into society. The community tradition worked better than any modern forms of psychotherapy..."

As I reflected on this article, the Holy Spirit revealed that there were spiritual truths in action. These truths led to personal healing for Felfiel and for the community and provided a pathway for reconciliation. Felfiel chose to walk three days' journey to his village, the opposite direction from the war. This is repentance. He then submitted to his family and community by taking the *muti*. A combination of repentance, humility, and perhaps belief the *muti* would bring relief, prepared Felfiel for release from spiritual and natural torment. The community responded with forgiveness, and reconciliation occurred. I now look deeper into spiritual practices. The motivation or principle of behavior is more important than the method. Behaviors that foster life and healthy relationships are consistent with Scripture.

Projects in Sierra Leone were finished. Team members were tired, but grateful for connection with others for mutual and meaningful change. It was time to return to the *Africa Mercy*, docked in Conakry, Guinea. After settling in, the mental health team traveled to Kissidougou, a town in the north of Guinea. This remote location was chosen because so little training is offered far from the capital cities. The participants included church leaders, teachers, one military officer, and a police chief.

The military officer sat on the last row and the police chief on the first row, neither of them interacting with other participants. The church leaders knew each other and dialogued freely, as did the teachers. At break time I said to the police chief, "You have a difficult job." He nodded in the affirmative. I said, "I have a difficult job, too. But if it was easy, everyone would do it."

His demeanor changed; he realized someone knew how he felt, recognized the weight he carried and reassured him he was valued and not invisible. I said this to make connection, but that doesn't make it any less true. I don't manipulate or flatter but speak what I truly believe. In the process, I am also strengthened and sometimes exhorted.

The mental health team strives to equip all provider groups, especially church leaders. One of these leaders said, "You have found a way to share the gospel without making people angry." The team desires to bring hope and healing through every avenue possible—with Jesus as the center. God opens doors and gives us the opportunity not only to increase mental health capacity in nations, but as said before, to plant spiritual seeds.

A wrinkle emerged when the team returned to the ship in May 2013. Going forward, the mental health team was not only limited to short-term projects but must also be housed off the ship. The program had already released its long-term beds for hospital crew, and now I struggled over being permanently separated from community. I had served on board the ships intermittently since 1999. A million thoughts went through my head. I reeled from the sudden upheaval, blindsided by the news. A friend onboard said, "It's not over until it's over," but I knew God discouraged me from fighting. He had control. He could open the door if He chose to do so. But He didn't.

My heart, and some of my belongings, remained onboard. Is it possible to sustain an off-ship program with no place to store supplies and no well-maintained vehicles? The decision raised many questions, and I grieved the loss. Yet, I would make my best effort to keep the program alive.

I informed the mental health team and reminded them that we hold plans loosely. I told the story of how God created an egg for me for Jeff's graduation cake. God provides, and He sustains His plan. I attended a community meeting and escaped into Chris Tomlin's song "Lay Me Down." When we lay ourselves down, God lifts us up. I chose to "lay me down," submitting my plans and my life to God's sovereignty. *You are so good, God. You know exactly how to change our perspective to line up with your purposes.* I packed my belongings, hoping it was temporary. Yet not my will, but God's will be done.

Projects would continue with Mercy Ships, but the process changed to the mental health team traveling before and after the ship to increase visibility and build healthy relationships. Mercy Ships hoped to include more off-ship teams. Protocols are signed with countries months to years before a Mercy Ship arrives, and small projects provide for early engagement in upcoming countries. I accepted that mental health programming would not serve alongside the ship and prepared to venture into new territory. Taking a summer break in Texas would give me time to regroup and wait for the Holy Spirit to direct the next steps.

I left the *Africa Mercy* and returned to the US with mixed feelings. Sad to leave yet not perplexed. I rearranged my storage unit, determined to run the race unimpeded by external or internal baggage. My storage unit and my car held everything I owned. I could restructure the Mental Health Program once I settled for three months near my home church in Virginia.

Driving restores me. During hours on the road, I recount God's goodness, reflecting on His past faithfulness and on His present direction. I knew my time at Mercy Ships was not over but pondered how I might expand the Mental Health Program with limited resources. I was forty-five when I joined Mercy Ships. Could I adjust and keep the pace at sixty-two?

I encouraged myself by remembering the trials I had navigated in the past. All of them led to greater opportunity and a deeper sense of my calling to love God, others, and myself. I chose to embrace this detour, convinced God was not finished with me yet. Ultimately, it's not my opinion that matters. What does God want me to do? My voyage, though fraught with pitching and rolling, must connect with God's direction. Otherwise, my work is meaningless.

Proverbs 16:9 reads, "In their hearts humans plan their course, but the Lord establishes their steps." I certainly know how to plan, often years in advance. Yet I have learned to say, "God willing," I will do this, or I will do that. Nothing is under my control. Life becomes less of a struggle as I surrender my personal agenda to our omniscient, omnipotent, and omnipresent Father.

Chapter Eighteen

Imprisoned

I had a mammogram before I left Texas on my way to Virginia. Not long after, I received a letter recommending a biopsy. Through prayer, I suspected positive results of breast cancer, so I prepared myself for the news.

Yet life goes on. I traveled to attend a birthday celebration for a friend in the Allegheny and Blue Ridge Mountains. Though it was her birthday, she gave each of us a journal with a Scripture inside the hand-knitted cover. My Scripture, Philippians 4:13, reads, "I can do all this through him who gives me strength."

I rose early to see the sun inch its way gently over the mountains. The air was crisp, and pink-tinged clouds penetrated the sky. The experience triggered memories of my visit to the Sistine Chapel. Michelangelo spent backbreaking hours painting the finger of God reaching out to the finger of man. I walked through the Stations of the Cross later that day and remembered God's sacrifice. Pictures of Jesus with the crown of thorns on his head, his side pierced, and the curtain of the temple torn in two, etched themselves in my mind. I pondered the crown of thorns as I made the return trip back to my church home.

I told my pastor that I expected the biopsy to be positive for cancer. He paused for a moment; then said, "Paul wrote from prison." Always the optimist. Always the encourager. Ever able to see beyond the natural with the mind of Christ. Pastors Ken and Holly have been bulwarks of faith and solid encouragers for me since I joined the church in 1992. I thank God for placing me in a loving and safe sanctuary that fosters personal and ministry growth.

Life experience taught me that a rolling stone gathers no moss. I dared not focus on "what if" since research suggests people worry approximately 80 percent of the time without cause. I made and delivered gingerbread houses to a few friends, combining my love of making them with my love of giving. One house was designed for a couple I admire and trust for their spiritual depth, persistent faith, and uncompromising love for me. The atmosphere was perfect, a chill in the air but a cozy fire by the water. We prayed for healing and for me to increase in the power of supernatural healing. They prayed my words would become words of wisdom and God-given creativity. That I may dodge the obstacles and keep moving forward in wisdom and supernatural gifts.

On my way to the clinic, the Holy Spirit said, "Finally, be strong in the Lord and in his mighty power," (Ephesians 6:10) and "No weapon forged against you will prevail … This is the heritage of the servants of the Lord, and this is their vindication from me,' declares the Lord." (Isaiah 54:17).

When I arrived at the clinic, the nurse gave me a bottle of water and set me at a table. I listened carefully to the physician. "You do have cancer, but it will not be the cause of your death. Please see a surgeon, and we will also schedule you with an oncologist and a radiologist to see if chemotherapy and/or radiation is necessary." I thanked them for the information. They were surprised I was calm, but the Holy Spirit had prepared me for the news ahead of time.

My pastor and his mother-in-law took me for surgery and stayed throughout. What an amazing church I have—how precious is the body of Christ. Many friends saw me through the initial days, and Jeff visited me in Virginia to accompany me to the radiologist appointment. I planned to stay in Virginia until mid-March, when radiation would end. My wings were clipped! I was in prison.

> In all this you greatly rejoice, though now for a little while you may have had to suffer grief in all kinds of trials. These have come so that the proven genuineness of your faith—of greater worth than gold, which perishes even though refined by fire—may result in praise, glory and honor when Jesus Christ is revealed. Though you have not seen him, you love him; and even though you do not see him now, you believe in him and are filled with an inexpressible and glorious joy, for you are receiving the end result of your faith, the salvation of your souls. (I Peter 1:6-9)

May my faith be proven genuine.

Radiation Technicians marked my body with tattoos for radiation, and treatments were planned five days a week for seven weeks. I had rarely returned to Virginia after leaving for Texas in 1996. Staying put gave me the opportunity to strengthen relationships and build new ones.

I went to Burger King before treatment started, and I saw no less than fifty children with crowns on their heads, laughing and singing. Patrons complained, and the staff apologized, but the sight of a room full of happy children made me laugh. They are children of the King, and I, too, am a child of the King. *Thank you, my King, for enduring the crown of thorns.* Isaiah 62:3 promises, "You will be a crown of splendor in the Lord's hand, a royal diadem in the hand of your God." Jesus promises a crown of splendor while He wore a crown of thorns. A favorite song came to mind as I pondered His immeasurable love.

> My Jesus, I love thee, I know thou art mine.
> To thee all the follies of sin I resign.
> I love thee for wearing the crown upon thy brow,
> If ever I loved thee, my Jesus tis now.

I saw the kind and compassionate oncologist after Christmas. I did not need chemotherapy, but she recommended ten years of anti-hormone treatment in addition to surgery and radiation. Following the oncologist's plan meant I would be seventy-four when the treatment ended. Side effects such as insomnia, hot flashes, bone loss, joint pain, blood clots, dry skin, weight gain, uterine cancer, and others were possible. I chose not to take the medication, with confirmation through prayer and my pastor's counsel. Better a shorter, productive life than a long unproductive one, complicated by multiple symptoms.

Total surrender was challenging as I completed radiation. Fatigue limited my physical activity, but the still small voice brought peace. I thanked God we had caught the cancer early, and the extra time allowed for thinking outside of the box. What if I expanded mental health programming globally? I was drawn from childhood to serve on multiple continents. In recent years, Mercy Ships has focused its service to Africa, so I considered other options.

Friends of Touch was a 501(c)(3) faith-based organization, birthed through my church. It existed to provide support for an organization called Touch (The Outreach to Unfortunate Children's Hurts). Touch provided education and meals to impoverished children in Kampala, Uganda, with most children coming from single-parent homes. Perhaps it would serve the world better by changing its direction toward community development, including mental health. Kay Helm, the director of Friends of Touch, along with other team members and I, met to pray through the next steps.

Part of the transition suggested changing the name. What would serve the mission well? One team member suggested the name Tributaries International. Tributaries indicates not only living water flowing downward (from God to and through us to others), but also multiple small channels going in many directions. Tributaries go down, go out, and return. Transformed lives then touch others. They become the tributaries. To give tribute means to act, say, or do something to show gratitude, respect, or admiration. The Tributaries team follows God with reverence and desires to see His kingdom come on earth. Habakkuk 2:14 reads, "For the earth will be filled with the knowledge of the glory of the LORD as the waters cover the sea." Mercy Ships and Tributaries would collaborate on mental health projects to fulfill Habakkuk 2:14.

Seven weeks later, radiation was complete. I wrote in my journal, "Thank you for being with me in my treatment. I believe you give life and Satan takes life. But I am thankful you are a Redeemer and use the circumstances of loss to bring healing in other ways, and to transform us to your likeness." The radiation team gave me a little ceremony where I rang the bell (getting my wings), a certificate, and an angel figurine that read, "Faith makes all things possible." They had been lovely, and to my joy, my wings were no longer clipped.

The word *gauntlet* originated from a Swedish word from the 1600s, *gatlopp*, which means lane-course. It referred to a form of military punishment where a man ran between two rows of soldiers who struck him with sticks or knotted ropes. Survival depends on running the race with your eye on the goal, not distracted by obstacles. My gauntlet required that I lay down my will, my desires, and my plans. Distractions might become a snare. If the mental health team had gone on to the next field service with the *Africa Mercy*, I would have ignored nudges to get a mammogram. The invisible enemy cancer might have spread. We make plans with limited perspective, so I must trust Him when things don't go the way I want them to. God knew the future. He watched over me, as He has done my entire life. God frustrates our plans to bring His purposes to pass. He thwarts our plans as a loving and protective Father.

Walking out my own cancer journey was so much easier than walking with Jeff through his. It is mentally and emotionally agonizing to stand by while the child you gave birth to suffers extreme physical and emotional wounds. Thoughts of powerless and hopelessness creep in and require soothing through the Holy Spirit. God had healed Jeff ten years before, and I trusted the Son of Righteousness would come with healing in His wings for me, too. "But I have calmed and quieted my soul, like a weaned child with its mother; like a weaned child is my soul within me" (Psalm 131:2 ESV).

Treatment was completed, and I needed to decide whether I would return to Guinea as planned or take the safer path and remain in the United States. Traveling in low-and-middle-income countries creates all sorts of issues, but West Africa was facing an epidemic ravaging the nations of Sierra Leone, Liberia, and Guinea. Ebola, a deadly virus spread through contact with body fluids, caused rapid death; I was immunocompromised following radiation, and travel to Guinea would put my health at risk. Catastrophic levels of fear of Ebola escalated on all fronts, affecting people both at home and abroad.

I faced three challenges: 1) Mercy Ships made daily decisions on whether team members could travel to Guinea; 2) I questioned if I was prepared to die due to Ebola, since I had just fought to live through cancer; and 3) I wondered, should I survive, if there would be somewhere for me to stay when I returned home. Following God's direction to give up a regular place of residence comes with challenges most people aren't aware of. I chose to travel to Guinea once Mercy Ships gave approval.

Touching down in Conakry, Guinea, I experienced a dramatic shift in atmosphere from the previous year. No one shook hands, terrified that it meant death. Joy and excitement were absent, contrary to Guineans' friendly nature. West Africa had never experienced Ebola before—11,325 people died. Most people did not trust health care workers and considered them disease carriers, which led to some health workers being killed by people overcome with fear. Quarantine areas were built for those exposed to the virus. Panicked family members hid their dead, with unresolved grief the result.

My choice to travel to Guinea when others hoped to escape opened the hearts of the mental health workshop participants. When I left, the police chief escorted me to the airport, pushed my luggage trolley and said, "Thank you for coming to Guinea when others are trying to get out." When he said goodbye at the ticket counter, the attendant exchanged my economy seat for a business-class ticket.

"Thank you, Jesus" I said. Once onboard, I began a conversation with the woman sitting next to me. I remarked how thankful I was for the business-class seat.

She replied, "Yes, we give business-class seats to Mercy Ships crew whenever they are available, for their generosity to our country." I took a deep breath, then smiled. Both Mercy Ships and I received the favor of God.

The trip to Guinea gave me an opportunity to analyze my motives for traveling to potentially dangerous locations. Do I go for the thrill, or do I go because I wholeheartedly follow the road God sets before me? This specific trip post-cancer gave me clarification. I go where most people don't go to carry Jesus to remote and desperate places less exposed to the gospel. Some destinations hold danger because of war and violence, while some hold danger due to illness and disease. Both are life-threatening.

> Then Jesus said to His disciples, If anyone desires to be My disciple, let him deny himself [disregard, lose sight of, and forget himself and his own interests] and take up his cross and follow Me [cleave steadfastly to Me, conform wholly to My example in living and, if need be, in dying, also]. (Matthew 16:24, AMPC)

I lived out the Chutes and Ladders game during 2013–2014. Ups and downs, twists and turns, one step forward, one step back. I faced my own life-threatening illness, then plunged headfirst into the Ebola-ridden nation of Guinea. Somehow, my small life became less self-focused as I looked at devastation on a grand scale.

This season brought the worst and the best experiences. From pincushion to world traveler, I knew God treasured me. He sees me as a gem, hand-carved and prepared for the opportunities and challenges He puts before me. He drew me out of many waters and lifted me from darkness into His protective care. I didn't need to know how He would do it or where He was taking me. I needed to rest in His capable arms and watch the miracle happen.

I'm often asked how I cope surrounded by grief and trauma day after day. Jesus takes my pain and sorrow and fills my life with good things in pleasant places. I cope because of God's grace and His unfathomable love for suffering people. I see more than their pain. I see God reaching out with love and mercy. I feel His touch when

He tenderly applies the balm of Gilead. I hear His gentle voice calling people closer—calling them deeper. I smell the sweet fragrance of love. God shows me the beauty in them and His plan for healing and redemption. I'm not a bystander to His grace, but rather a partner in it. As He ministers, I stand in awe.

Though briefly imprisoned, the journey bubbles over with adventure. God created me for this. I am running down the road with no end in sight. Little by little, He delivers me. I am no longer haunted by darkness and demons, but I face darkness in greater measure each year. Little by little, He grows my faith; my trust; my courage; my confidence. I am His, and He is mine.

Chapter Nineteen

"Regardez-Moi"

Having navigated ministry redirection, cancer, Ebola, and war-torn countries over the previous fifteen months, I paused to consider my next steps. I loved to read as a child and teenager and did so often when I wasn't scurrying from one activity to another. I delved into fantasies and allegories and read many of the classics, which elude me now. I occasionally dabbled in writing fiction and poems and had an inkling that one day I would write books. Earlier nudges to write, previously tucked away, became more frequent, more intense, and more urgent. Writing now preoccupied my thoughts.

His love is deeper, wider, higher than what we can imagine, and so are His purposes. Though my primary purpose is to bring healing to suffering people, writing brings healing through another stream of ministry. I'd coauthored other materials and had several book ideas germinating when inspiration for a new children's healing book came from an unexpected source.

A friend and I traveled to the small town of Uncertain, Texas, on an ordinary summer day. We planned an outing on the *Graceful Ghost*, a motorboat exploring Caddo Lake. Captain Ron steered the boat through the peaceful, yet slightly ominous waters while I disappeared on the surreal journey steeped in mystery. We marveled at the cypress trees, turtles, birds, and even the parasites devouring the lake. My friend wanted to see an alligator. Captain Ron said, "I have ten alligators. Do you want to see them?" Who agrees to go with a stranger to see his alligators? But we went, looking forward to the adventure.

I saw three birds when we entered the living room. A small yellow bird sat motionless on her perch. Capt. Ron had named her Baby. The trembling bird belonged to his aunt who died a few months before. Baby pined profoundly, alone in the house for a week after the aunt died. It brought back memories of my mother, a hemiplegic, lying in bed, unable to move, when my stepfather died quietly in another room. My mother lay there for three days, terrified he abandoned her. Both my mother and Baby experienced the unthinkable—cries without response in a dreary, grey, and empty room.

The second bird, Caesar, appeared small in stature, but had a loud, piercing voice. Caesar was annoying and squawked endlessly. He flapped his wings in a frenzy and seemed determined to steal the peaceful day from me.

The third bird, a large, majestic parrot named Grace, sat upright, with dignity and strength. Grace said over and over, "Hello. Hello. Hello," and "Welcome." Just like our Heavenly Father, saying "Hello" and "Welcome" to the world; over and over, and over again. Waiting. His patience and grace—amazing. His wisdom—unfathomable. His love—evident in His bittersweet death on the cross. Bitter for Him—sweet for us. Grace ushered me from the chaos of Caesar's world back to peace.

My friend and I joined Captain Ron behind his house, where the alligators and other unique animals lived. Our God is generous. As Ron promised, we saw ten tenacious alligators. Captain Ron said the alligator is a sprinter. He will catch you, but his distance is just 75 feet, and he only runs straight. He can't maneuver his body if you shift directions, darting right and left. I thought about the journey of faith and the obstacles along our paths. We must be wise as serpents and harmless as doves to confuse and outmaneuver our spiritual enemies rather than be outmaneuvered by them. A seemingly ordinary and uncertain day became a day of outlandish surprises and deep reflection.

A year later, Mercy Ships and Tributaries partnered together for another project in Benin, West Africa. I chose to spend the weekend in my room since I had seen the tourist areas in the past. This room was in an unusual setting—the waste management administration building for a local hospital. A few rooms had been built dormitory style to host traveling team members. But since the building housed administrative offices, and no one worked on weekends, only a lone guard stood watch at the front door. Kay and I were essentially tucked away.

The Holy Spirit reminded me of the three birds from Uncertain, Texas, and I began to form a storyline. The isolation and quiet setting provided a perfect place to start the new book for grief and trauma healing in children. I realized birds apply to all demographics. Any age group, any culture, any gender, can relate to birds. I wanted to create something with low production costs that could be used in a simple setting.

Much of my work occurs in Africa, so I chose birds common to West Africa (the canary) and Central Africa (the grey parrot). All the characters in the story are named after my team members or their wives; except for the birds, who already had names when I met them. I wrote a basic story, with activities, Scriptures, and prayers to be shared with children over two long weekends or a seven-week period. Thoughts came quickly, and I completed the first draft in about five hours. Nestled in my freezing but cozy dorm room, I settled on *Baby Finds Grace* as the title.

Writing a book intended to bring healing to anyone carries high accountability and responsibility. But writing a book to work with vulnerable children is even more critical and requires care with deep sensitivity to protect their minds and hearts. We incorporated *Baby Finds Grace* into the program.

I identify with hurting children since my own childhood and young adult years were laced with trauma. What happened to me and to countless others breaks God's heart, and He longs to bring healing. But healing does not depend solely on Jesus and others. Each person must believe life and relationships can be restored and must have the courage to heal.

Children find some degree of healing through the process of telling their stories, but also from hearing the stories of others. After reading *Baby Finds Grace*, one of the children said, "Baby knows how I feel." Knowing someone else suffered pain helps people of any age recognize they are not alone.

At times I share my story with the children, and it opens their minds and hearts to believe that one day they too might heal. Service providers receive a level of healing themselves as they learn new ways to help the children. Many children do not willingly share their stories. It takes intentionality for teachers to go beyond the classroom and get to know the stories of the children they serve. With this, comes great responsibility. Children may share stories of abuse, which then requires the service provider, whether it's a teacher, a spiritual leader, or a health care worker, to take steps to protect the child. Otherwise, the child has opened an area of pain without a road to healing.

Pictures tell a thousand words. I asked a small group to draw a picture of something that reminds them of a painful experience. One young girl drew a picture of a pencil. She said that one day she forgot her pencil, and the headmaster caned her. Three of the other five children said they had been caned for the same reason.

I asked the headmaster if our team could meet with him and the teachers the next day for training. He agreed. During training, I questioned how they were disciplined as a child, how they want children to remember them, and how they want to be seen by the community. Faces were somber as they reflected on the past and considered the present. After training the school staff on other ways to discipline and help children grow, the headmaster said, "We just didn't know what else to do."

Of all the stories, one has been the most difficult for me to process. I offered a children's workshop with a group of children, and one child (I'll call her Hawah) isolated herself completely. When the children played games, Hawah sat alone on a bench with her head down to avoid interaction. During small group discussions,

Hawah sat quietly, listened to the other children's stories, but was unwilling to share her own.

My co-facilitator and I met privately with Hawah, who shared her story in whispers with tears. A few years before, Hawah was very hungry and stole a small amount of money from her parents to buy some bread. When the parents learned the money was gone, they locked Hawah in a room. They poured gasoline on Hawah's hands and arms and set them on fire. Amid the screams, her parents poured more gasoline and lit the fire again. This resulted in scars and limited the use of her hands. Also, the parents were put in prison. Thus, Hawah lost not only the use of her hands but also her family. Hawah received some emotional healing during the group and began to play with other children.

The next year, the team brought the children together for follow-up. I used "peeps" of different colors, and stuffed animals of different shapes, sizes and designs to demonstrate that each one of us is unique yet perfect in the eyes of God. Hawah listened intently, then told me I could share her drawing and her story if it would help protect other children. A greater level of healing had taken place.

Many children take what they learn during the workshop and share it with other children in their homes, neighborhoods, or schools. Some change is dramatic and immediate; some change takes time. We can't improve family system issues in one week, but we can help children cope with their circumstances in a healthier way and heal some wounds of the past. This makes the workshops worthwhile.

Listening to children's pain, anyone's pain, hurts. Oh, that we lived in a perfect world without suffering and trauma. Scripture reminds us that those who accept Jesus will be with Him in heaven, where there is no more sorrow. Revelation 21:4 reads, "He will wipe every tear from their eyes. There will be no more death, or mourning or crying or pain, for the old order of things has passed away." We long for that day but live in the present.

I can't always protect these little ones from pain, but I can help them navigate to the other side. I can lead workshops for children to learn coping skills and to find their own voice. I can pray for Jesus to heal their hearts, intercede on their behalf, and show Himself faithful in both His love and His presence.

I remembered one child saying, *"Regardez-moi !"* which means, "Look at me! See me!" I pray *Baby Finds Grace* is a catalyst for children of any age to be seen—to be loved.

PART FIVE.
STORIES FROM THE NATIONS

Chapter Twenty

Jerusalem, Judea, Samaria and the World

By 2015, my hopes and dreams of bringing much-needed mental health services to an underserved world had become a reality. I reflected on a trip to Geneva in the early 1980s. I had made a specific detour to view the World Health Organization complex and hoped one day I might be part of a global medical organization like the WHO. I had no expectations, only hopes and dreams. God changed incidental moments into seeds of faith, watered them, and then watched them bloom through action.

I considered my initial journey toward missions and had no idea of the scope or complexities of what lay before me. Challenges and obstacles multiplied exponentially. Ignorance is bliss. I believe God gives us just enough vision to move us forward, and not enough to frighten us away. Stretching is painful, but profitable in the long run.

Short mission trips on the continents of Asia, North and Central America, the Middle East, and Europe were opportunities to get my feet wet but not become deeply immersed in cultures. Entering Mercy Ships provided a sound structure, a strong community, and an understanding of organizational development from missional, health care, and maritime perspectives and experience in partnering with governmental ministries. This foundation allowed me to step out with greater confidence as I entered new territories without the structural support of a global charity. I continue to find my feet as I trust God to open doors, yet close doors He wants closed.

The Holy Spirit spoke to me in a worship service about five years ago. "The world is open to you. You can go anywhere you want." He caught my attention, and I was both delighted and pensive. The "world" is massive, and so are the needs. Expansion demands responsibility, integrity, excellence. Yet it is this opening and closing of doors that allows me to continue to live out my God-given purpose—bringing hope and healing to people through direct mental health care, and by training other people around the world to increase capacity. I continue to need someone stronger than me to climb ever-increasing mountains, to dig my way out of dark pits, and to accompany me through miles and miles of wilderness.

A major challenge during the previous ten years was developing mental health materials that would not only be holistic, but applicable across the globe. One complication is the interface between Scripture and cultures. Not only are cultures limitless, but some (or some portions of them) are antithetical to Scripture. I approached this topic with a bishop from Mozambique. I said, "What do you do when Scripture and culture collide?"

He responded, "Scripture wins." His definitive response solidified my determination to not shy away from cultural issues that polarize people but to seek ways to bridge the gap with Jesus as the center.

Initially, I used separate content for formal and informal service providers. The book *Healing the Wounds of Trauma: How the Church Can Help,* written by SIL and Wycliffe, is easy to understand, spiritually rich, and integrates whole person care. I chose to expand the content to include a basic understanding of people, and specific information on mental health, neurological and substance use disorders.

Other material I used from *Where There is No Psychiatrist* for formal service providers was helpful but limited in that it did not include diagnoses or a spiritual perspective. Clinicians found it confusing since they were aware of diagnoses but didn't know how to assess or treat them. Discussing situations and symptoms without providing actual diagnosis was not helpful in the clinics where I served.

The WHO developed an additional area of content in 2010: *The Mental Health Gap Intervention Guide* (mhGAP-IG). While this, too, lacked spiritual content, it was developed with over sixty global mental health professionals who intentionally wrote materials to increase capacity by training primary health care workers in low-and-middle-income countries.

Developing and implementing the Mental Health Program over fifteen years gave me the opportunity to integrate content from all three areas, including my own materials created from over fifty years of practice. *Understanding People, Mental Health and Trauma (UPMHT)* is divided into five parts. The five models (Whole Person, Maslow's Hierarchy of Needs, Johari Window, Behavior Process Model, and the Change Model) have now become The Westman Framework, an umbrella perspective integrated throughout the manual. What began as a handful of individual resource materials has now become a manual of over 250 pages.

My goal was to understand people from a holistic perspective, rather than through a single lens such as medical, psychological, social or spiritual. If service providers seek to understand the story rather than make decisions based only on behavior, people will be better served. Many participants say the content is easy to understand and to implement. Some report previous training (even college or university level) taught them theory, but they didn't know what to do with it.

The workshop Is designed to facilitate content in one language over forty hours. The mental health team travels to the location and offers training over one week, since it is more cost effective to do so. Those who have had training and are both proficient and interested are able to spread training over several weeks or months since they do not have the same time constraints. Workshops typically include 30–40 participants seated at tables of four to six for small group interaction.

A major issue became how to accurately translate the manual into additional languages. Resources I used previously were already translated into French, but after expansion to nations other than English- or French-speaking, new translations were required. Many colleagues admit that accurate translation is a major hurdle, and inaccurate translation in the field of mental health can be life-threatening for people in severe situations. Competent translators were needed for Asia, the Middle East, and Central and South America.

Another hurdle is that some participants may not speak the identified language even though they were told ahead of time which language would be spoken. Our team might be told the group speaks French, and on arrival we learn some speak a tribal language, or they speak French or Spanish as a second language and want an English book. This requires two interpreters to represent the different language groups. We are not prepared for these situations, and it leads to confusion and a less-than-ideal learning environment.

Baby Finds Grace (BFG) is included in most training workshops, unless the project is shortened, or the participants have no plan to work with children. This book, too, must be accurately translated and implemented.

A mental health project team typically has from one to four facilitators. Six people have served with the Mental Health Program for more than ten years, and they all continue to join the team on some projects. Naomi, Samuel, Soule, Kay, Torbjoerg, and Georges are team members who know the content and who adjust easily with changing logistics. I depend on them to maintain unity; a united team can withstand anything that attacks from without. And they lift my arms by thinking the best of me when stress highlights my imperfections.

Short-term team members are added based on education, faith, location, language, time of year, country dynamics, and the team member's own schedule since all of them have other positions. Each team is unique.

Mercy Ships serves only in Africa, but a growing number of partners offer projects on every continent. As a result, in any given year, projects may be implemented in several locations, which allows for more team members to participate and for more people served around the world. The harvest is plentiful, and the workers are few; especially in faith-based mental health. Open doors complicate logistics but bring a greater sense of purpose.

When asked what it's like to be in full-time missions, I say, "It's challenging but fulfilling. I am privileged to travel the world for the sake of the gospel." Missionaries understand sacrifice is a given; but seasoned ones also know we can't outgive God. I am amazed He opens ever-increasing doors with both nations and partners. Capacity grows, and more people are healed. And each country gives me greater appreciation for the Creator and His creation.

The Westman Framework

Whole Person Model

Where does the problem originate, and how is each area affected?

BODY	SOUL Mind-Emotions-Will
SPIRIT	SOCIAL RELATIONSHIPS

Maslow's Hierarchy of Needs (adapted)

What need or needs is the person trying to meet?

Johari Window

Who is aware of the problem?

	Known to Self	Not Known to Self
Known to Others	ARENA	BLIND SPOT
Not Known to Others	FAÇADE	UNKNOWN

Behavior Process Model

Why does the person do what he/she does?

SITUATION → THOUGHTS → FEELINGS → ACTIONS/ BEHAVIORS → SITUATION

Change Model

Where is the person in the change process?

AWARENESS → MOTIVATION → KNOWLEDGE & SKILLS → ENERGY → HOPE

Naomi

Torbjoerg

Samuel

Soulé

Kay

Georges

Chapter Twenty-One

Asia

I climbed the Buddhist high place in 1996 and eagerly awaited an opportunity to return to Asia. My church, LightHouse, connected me with one of our missionaries, Scott. Our team joined him in India to provide crisis counseling for orphans and staff who worked with children rescued from human trafficking. Both children and staff suffered from emotional wounds, and we provided care as best we could in a short period of time. Collaboration with Scott continues across nations and continents.

Nepal

Scott connected the mental health team with one of his partners in Nepal just after the 2015 earthquake. Scott saw the need for mental health training after approximately 9,000 people died from the 7.8 magnitude quake. The project was planned, but travel was complicated due to strikes over a new constitution. Motorbikes and rickshaws rather than cars zig-zagged down the road, requiring travel by rickshaw through heavy rains all week.

The political climate deteriorated. After dinner on the final night, we traveled on motorbikes back to the hotel. Police cars with megaphones had announced an 8:00 p.m. curfew, but we didn't hear it. Near the main street, just a block from our hotel, a policeman told us to turn around and use back roads. He said, "We have authority to shoot." So, turn around we did. It seemed more dangerous to travel the dark back roads; but we had no choice. This time I felt afraid. We learned that twenty-two policemen had been killed approximately 140 kilometers from us. There was reason for high security. Yet again, training occurred during a crisis event. Reading about or watching emergency situations is much different than living them, for both participants and team members.

Terri, director of Second Chances, has been a friend for many years and traveled with our team as a short-term facilitator. Women identified with Terri as she shared her story of pain and victory.

> I was cruising through mid-life feeling loved, supported and serving the Lord with joy. Then one day, my life as I knew it was over. My heart was broken and shattered into a million pieces when my spouse abruptly ended our relationship. I was in shock and felt as if I had lost my identity. I did not know who I was or what my purpose was anymore. I did not know how to stop the unbearable pain of betrayal and rejection. I cried to the Lord for a miracle, or to take me home with Him, but He did not answer those prayers. During those desperate moments I realized this was just a hint of the pain Jesus felt when he was betrayed by his disciples.
>
> The Lord has used the pain and sorrow in my life and turned it into a conduit of compassion, mercy, grace, and unconditional love for other women whose lives have been broken and shattered. Thirteen years later, I am now serving in full-time ministry. Not only did the Lord restore me, but He gave me the desires of my heart. When I thought I was broken beyond repair, the Lord orchestrated a divine appointment with Lyn, and I will be forever grateful for her obedience to help bring healing in my life. Generations will be impacted by this simple act of obedience. I have learned God uses all our life experiences for his glory. Nothing was wasted.

I have been blessed by Terri's huge heart for suffering people, her generosity, but perhaps greatest of her gifts, her faith. She believes God for the impossible. Terri's vision was to open a rehabilitation center for those addicted to substances, and a self-sustaining resale store to make it a reality. Terri built a non-profit organization, purchased land, opened the store, provides services for people in need, and is opening a residence for rehabilitation.

Our small team then traveled to Kathmandu to train another group of church leaders. I was stunned by the gold-tinged beauty of the Himalayas as we flew parallel to them for much of an hour. Kathmandu, one of my favorite cities, is mystical and surreal.

With the backdrop of mountains, the old historic city is reminiscent of centuries gone by. Cobblestone streets, rickshaws, and Nepali music captured our senses. Kathmandu was less populated in September, since intermittent torrential rain prevented tourists from trekking. Lovely people; lovely culture. Smiles are large and inviting in Nepal; this makes it easier for merchants to charm tourists when they barter. People are warm and enjoy engaging in banter. Merchants are hospitable and offer tea to make time for a chat once you connect.

Nepal was our first training in a country where participants sat on the floor, with no shoes, for an entire week. They were eager to learn. One participant said he learned not to throw stones at people with severe mental disorders, and he would discourage others from doing so. We don't judge cultural practices. People do what they learn from others. We help them see things differently and grow in the process. We grow as well. Team members endeavor to learn more about the culture and about typical behaviors wherever we go.

The team flew to Chitwan National Park for a rest, but no one met us at the airport. Terri called the hotel, then we heard her say, "A horse cart? You're coming to get us on a horse cart?" We dragged our luggage across the street to buy a cold drink and waited for transportation. The temperature was 115 degrees Fahrenheit, and the horse cart picked us up 1 ½ hours later. We rode eighteen kilometers on paved and dirt roads, hearing only "Clip Clop, Clip Clop." I heard the sound in my sleep for months afterward. We traveled on no fewer than twelve different modes of transportation, including canoes, an ox, and an enormous elephant.

During the visit to Chitwan, I had an opportunity for a perspective change. Tigers inhabit Chitwan National Park, so I prayed to see one on the elephant ride. Our three-person team climbed onto the back of the elephant, with our feet hanging down, in the seat made for four people. Two faced forward and one faced toward the rear of the elephant. I saw women in the grasslands pulling herbs for dinner. The same day, a woman was killed by a tiger while gathering herbs to cook a special dinner for her husband returning from a long journey. It made me think. My unimportant desires trigger simple prayers. If God fulfills my desire, it may mean death to someone else. God has a perfect answer for each prayer lifted to Him, yet I want to be more careful when I pray. I receive comfort knowing the woman was not killed in the area where we took our elephant ride. But she could have been. May I direct my prayers wisely and consider God knows better than I do.

Torbjoerg continues to serve on the mental health team but is also involved in many countries with other organizations. She is a talented psychiatrist and specializes in working with young males with schizophrenia. Torbjoerg's greatest gift, however, is that she genuinely loves people and life. She connected me with one of her Nepali partners who has a mental disorder and who built a mental health treatment facility. He deeply understands the suffering it causes, and treating this population gained him not only national, but international acclaim.

The partner brought a patient who wrote a song about living with a mental disorder. He sang of his longing to be accepted, not isolated and ostracized. The stones people hurl at him cause physical pain and emotional pain from rejection and abandonment.

> Nabolau Malai Pagaal Bhani[4]
>
> Do not call me mad, I have a mind like yours.
> Do not hit with stones calling me mad; I have feelings like yours.
> The shadow is mine, why do blood relations also become strangers.
> The hills and mountains where yesterday I played,
> Why! It has become so far away.
> I do not want property; I only want your perception to be changed.
> I did not ask for stars of the sky, Only I ask for the right to live.
> Do not call me mad, I have a mind like yours.
> Do not hit with stones, calling me mad; I have feelings like yours.

The participants sat quietly. I thanked the patient who shared his story and said, "Now we've heard how it feels to be on the other end of the stone." I was able to tell him the participants no longer throw stones and have increased awareness about how the stigma of mental disorders causes pain. God's heart breaks for those considered outcasts. Jeremiah 30:17 reads, "'But I will restore you to health and heal your wounds,' declares the Lord, 'because you are called an outcast, Zion for whom no one cares.'" His song never grows old to me. I hold back tears as I remember Jesus healed my soul. I walked the same road many years ago.

We offered a project in Nuwakot, an area devastated by the earthquake the previous year. It was quite challenging for me to climb up and down the slippery, mud-covered mountain slope. I was wearing flip-flops, which allowed both mud and leeches to hitch a ride. One day a participant ran ahead of me and taunted, "I'm fifty-five and I can do it." Of course he could, since he spent his entire life on the mountain.

I replied, "Well, I'm sixty-five." The man looked stunned and never made another comment. While I'm not good at climbing, I won't give up. The victory is in the climb.

Training was offered in Pokhara, near the Himalayan Mountain range, and while there I visited with one of my Gurkha friends and his family. The quiet strength of the Gurkhas inspires me to grow. I began to understand the majesty of this formidable mountain range and its people as I lingered under Mount Annapurna. I imagined battles of long ago and considered the dramatic weather conditions. The Nepali people have learned to persevere through countless devastating events. At times, I am impatient rather than persevering. Spending time with Gurkhas strengthens my resolve.

Scott shares a situation that occurred during the mental health training he attended in Pokhara.

> "I just want to die" popped up on my screen from an old friend I had not been in touch with for years. I've worked with people as an ordained minister and missionary for decades, but the

> mental health training I was taking changed my approach to people. So, my mind started racing as I saw my friend's desperate message: "I just want to die." I realized I could not ignore him, so I messaged him right away. His wife had kicked him out, kept the children and all their money. I encouraged him, and he connected with a local pastor who met his immediate needs, which helped him choose life for himself and a future with his children. Lyn's training that day caused me to be proactive to help save my friend's life, and I'm thankful I had that opportunity.
>
> I've learned the training is an incredible way to get to the bottom of things in a relatively short amount of time. Soon after, I began teaching the course at a seminary in India to several groups of students; and they share personal issues with me and receive healing. Now many of those students, and others I've trained in Bangladesh, are in active ministry in different regions of India using what they've learned to help others.

Scott has served in India and the greater region for over thirty years. He has tremendous physical, social, and spiritual capacity, has a passion to preach, and lives life to the full. Scott is an optimist, and he challenges me to focus on opportunities rather than obstacles.

Myanmar (formerly Burma)

I was invited to a birthday party in Myanmar for Torbjoerg and thirty of her closest friends. Since I would be in Thailand on a YWAM project, it was a short flight to join her for a few days. I am always alert for potential mental health project opportunities, and I carried an email a pastor had sent to Tributaries some months earlier, asking for assistance for his orphanage. The pastor came to meet me at the hotel in Mandalay, and we made plans to visit the orphanage the following day. He and his wife, Hannah Lyn, picked me up and we traveled together to the tourist town of Pyin Oo Lwin. Hannah did not speak English but was attentive and smiled as we traveled the two hours to the home.

It was quite humbling to watch this couple serve sixty-four children with so little. I thought of the widow's mite, and how people will give everything they own to see God's kingdom come on earth as it is in heaven. Hannah Lyn is a young woman but has knots on her knees from praying. This, above all else, endeared her to me.

Mysterious Myanmar reminds me of ancient eras. This detour into the unknown included charming, quaint villages, visits to temples, and traveling the countryside by land and sea. Torbjoerg's birthday group took a boat to Inle Lake, where I had an amazing encounter.

While walking through a Buddhist temple, I saw a quiet young man absorbed in his craft. I noticed he had no hands and only one foot. He painted using the only human tool he had— his left foot. I was captivated.

I asked a nearby interpreter to learn his name and request permission to use his picture and story for my books. Kohtwe told her, "Yes. Soon I want to start a foundation. I hope to give half of my profit for other people like me." I learned the Kohtwe was born with no hands and only one foot.

I was struck by his generosity, since everyone else with a remarkable story of resilience wanted continued payment for their photo and story. I don't sell the manual, so it would be impossible for me to keep track of royalties. Just above his head, I saw a painting that would be perfect for the cover for *Understanding People, Mental Health, and Trauma*. By buying the painting, I found something I'd been looking for and was able to bless a man who sees the glass as half full instead of half empty. Kohtwe sees what he has, not what he doesn't have. He inspires me to do the same.

We were eventually able to hold two training workshops in Myanmar, including one near Inle Lake. Kohtwe visited the church leaders and humbly shared his story. Hannah Lyn and I took him home by boat, and he invited us in to meet his family. They asked Hannah Lyn to tell them her story, and she wept as she shared the gospel message. Her love for Jesus reaches to the innermost depths of her heart. The women then asked her to pray for them. Of course, she would; Hannah Lyn is an evangelist. The men sat quietly in the background as she prayed for the women. What was God doing in their hearts as she prayed? I hope to return one day and hear the rest of the story. Hannah Lyn inspires me with her passion, her simplicity, and her heart of gratitude.

Another man, a young evangelist, shared a powerful and insightful story during follow-up. In the past, when he entered a village, he would share the gospel and wait for a yes or no answer. If people refused the gospel message, he realized that he was no longer welcome. After training, he began to learn the stories of the people he met and how to identify and perhaps help with their felt needs. Now he is welcome in villages unconditionally. People may accept Jesus, and they may have their needs met. They may not. Either way, the evangelist is accepted. Through the training he learned to build relationships, and now doors remain open to him. He reminds me that all of us are evangelists when we sprinkle spiritual seeds. We are not responsible for the outcome. We just plant the seeds.

Cambodia

Tributaries connected with SEAPC, the ministry I traveled with to China in 1996. The founder's son, Matt Geppert, was now president. continuing in his father's global commitment to pray, meet the needs of people, and offer an encounter with Jesus. As the name declares, this global Christian community of friends believes that lives and nations are changed through prayer. SEAPC partners with local ministries in the platforms of healthcare, parenting, microeconomic development, and education. Matt asked me if Tributaries would offer mental health training for their children's homes workers across Cambodia and if we would be willing to start a children's healing workshop.

Cambodia, like countless other countries, faces a slow recovery from trauma. The civil war (1970–1975), followed by the brutal

Khmer Rouge Regime (1975–1979) left over one million people murdered, and countless children parentless. HIV infections following forced marriages increased the number of orphans. SEAPC has unique opportunities in this predominantly Buddhist nation to bring hope and healing in creative ways.

The mental health team offered workshops in both Phnom Penh and Siem Reap for the children's workers, followed by the workshop for children. I spent time with an orphaned child who suffered severe grief after losing her sister in a tragic accident. Tears surfaced as she shared her heart-wrenching story and the drawing she made of her sister.

This precious child touched me deeply. I asked permission to give a small piece of jewelry to this little angel. Asking permission is important because, as a guest, we must always leave decisions to those who have become the parents. Permission was granted, and I shared my tiny treasure with someone who needed it more than I did.

At the end of the day, the team walked to the car to return to the hotel. The child ran to me – stopped, looked intently into my eyes, and said, "I WILL remember you." Father, we are your hands, feet, and heart. May *Baby Finds Grace* comfort her as she finds You there.

The excursion in Cambodia was a sunrise visit to Angkor Wat, a temple complex that is considered the largest religious structure in the world. It was Hindu in origin but has been transformed into a Buddhist temple. Rising before dawn, our team arrived at the historical site and waited with anticipation. We were breathless as the sun spread its rays behind and to the sides of the myriads of temples and peaks. Jesus, reveal yourself as the Son of Righteousness coming with healing in your wings.

It was time to climb the steps to the temple. My two companions would climb; I vacillated. I knew the line of people moved steadily closer to the steps, and after entering, there was no turning back. The people walked single file up the steps without missing a beat. And then there was the steep yet rapid descent. Resolute I chose to make the round trip from bottom to top and back. I took one step, then another, then another. The line compressed halfway up, which gave me a few moments to catch my breath. We entered the temple; we looked; we prayed. And then we returned to the bottom. *Thank you, Jesus, I can still climb mountains. Bless the nation of Cambodia. Open doors for other countries in Asia, I pray.*

Chapter Twenty-Two

Pakistan

I developed mental health training for Pakistan at the request of a ministry partner located on the YWAM base near Mercy Ships. Their team had been asked to offer mental health training after a church was bombed in Peshawar. This ministry partner, Mercy Works, has an incredible ministry globally but provides direct care instead of mental health training. I met Brother James, who was the primary partner on the ground in Pakistan. An invitation was extended, and I considered it a privilege to join these heroes of faith.

Each person I ask shares a different perspective on Pakistan. Some recoil in horror or fear. Others become angry. Some express sadness and compassion toward those living in a war-torn land. Serving in Pakistan requires prayer and preparation, and assurance that God has called you to this global hotbed.

James met me after I cleared immigration. Two hours later, we arrived at a peaceful, snow-covered hideaway in the mountains, and I began the climb to the training center. The steps were crooked and slippery as I made my way up the mountain, with labored breathing due to the cold, thin air. I needed time to adjust to the altitude, so James suggested I lie down in my room for a slow transition.

I felt the first quake, and shortly thereafter, significant shaking of the room. I went outside and saw some participants running down the mountain to see if I was safe. No one was injured, but the training became more relevant in the middle of a life-threatening event as an 8.1 earthquake shook Afghanistan and northern Pakistan.

One week of training was a drop in the bucket. But one drop, then another, then another starts the flow of healing.

Our training site was located only twenty kilometers away from Abbottsford, where Osama Bin Laden was killed. People from surrounding areas, including Kashmir, Peshawar, and Lahore, came for the training. With the mountains of Kashmir as a backdrop, we mourned the tragedies of this disputed and devastated part of the world.

Training went well, building deep connections with these precious saints. I enjoyed my peaceful room. It was cold, even though I had warm water and a space heater. No one else had a heater; the young women slept together, huddled up to keep warm. They live in such meager conditions yet love Jesus with all their hearts. Though chilled to the bone physically, their selfless love warmed my heart.

Food was plentiful, and participants helped me get up and down the mountain steps, refusing to let me walk alone. They were humble and gentle servants. They smile, they give, they serve, and they are grateful for the smallest kindnesses shown them.

One participant shared her heart-wrenching story with me and gave permission for its inclusion here. Dina (not her real name) was betrayed by her husband, physically, mentally, emotionally abused, and kept away from her family. She had nowhere to go, little money, and a baby to care for. She wanted to die. Her grief was deep, but faith in God sustained her. Dina shared:

> "I knew I could trust you, and your prayers were powerful. The training makes a way in a sense that I've started to have a strength that I can stand. I can think positive. I can gather my pieces. I never knew before how many times I was traumatized, and I was never ever healed. But this training healed me. God showed me things and makes me stand at this very difficult time."

Dina reminds me how many people are isolated and hide their pain because of distrust, shame, or hopelessness. Everyone has a story, and I pray for greater awareness to seek others out and to be an encourager for them.

During the week, we went to see the oldest church in Pakistan. The quaint yet majestic building housed a very old register; the first page was signed by Queen Elizabeth and Prince Albert in 1947. My team member and I were given the honor of signing and were told we will be part of history. We walked through typical rural areas and an old school with a chapel. The mountains were breathtaking, towering over cities and towns.

There are constant struggles in the churches and for the population at large. Extremists do not discriminate when it comes to terrorizing people. Anyone is fair game. Women and children, civilians, and military are bombed with no remorse. Whatever is destroyed, whoever is hurt, is irrelevant—the perpetrator determines to create as much chaos, death, and destruction as possible.

Projects were offered in both Karachi and Lahore. Church leaders with rifles and AK-47s stood guard over the training venue, aware that attacks are unpredictable and occur without notice. There were ten terror attacks in eleven days during our training in this region; one just a few kilometers from the training.

A participant lost his close friend while we were training on trauma. I have worked in many war-torn countries, but this was the first time bombs exploded in the city, causing immediate and in-person trauma among our participants. Training becomes secondary when current grief and trauma occur by sudden death of a loved one. People gather. Genuine tears and compassion are the priority. Time stands still.

Internationals, especially Westerners, are high-risk targets. As a result, some hotels refused to give us rooms for fear that they might be vulnerable and in danger. As a result, the team stayed in a children's home, which caused our team stress over concern for the children. Though mindful of safety, we are not driven by it. We choose to be in the center of God's will, come what may. But mental health projects under these conditions are extremely intense and require constant concentration.

The mental health workshop closed with prayer. Participants were moved to tears as they expressed their pain and grief over the conditions in the nation, and particularly for the church. Those in dire circumstances are desperate for God. He meets them there. May we learn from them; their dependency on Jesus, knowing He is the One who brings healing. At the final ceremony, our team was given the Scripture Daniel 12:3: "Those who are wise will shine like the brightness of the heavens, and those who lead many to righteousness, like the stars for ever and ever." This is one of my life Scriptures. My heart was forever joined with the people of Pakistan.

The work in Pakistan has grown tremendously, and James founded an organization named The International Leadership Training

Institute (TILTI) in Islamabad. TILTI bridges service provider groups and nations together, now reaching beyond Pakistan into other territories.

A project was planned for fifty participants, but ninety-three attended, causing incredible stress for me. I want to bring healing and increase capacity for as many as possible, but I also want to keep numbers manageable for the best learning experience. How do I deny people access to training after persecution, martyred family members, torture, or death? Saying "no" to desperate people is difficult for me.

TILTI hires both Christians and Muslims and is strategic in seeking to foster peace in the region and beyond. Government leaders and leaders of other faith groups joined us for the final ceremony. I understand the mental health training opens additional doors for TILTI, and I am honored to be included as a faculty member. Participants were capable and some are now using *UPMHT* and *BFG* to provide training for others without requiring my presence. I am confident we will take the training to other territories and nations together.

I spent three nights with another group of DTS staff and students in the Pakistani mountains. On the first morning, I asked everyone to pray and ask God what He would like them to let go of. It could be anything—a thought, a behavior, an object. I then said I would like them to see how God brings healing in their lives by the end of the healing group. After some time, Thomas asked if he could leave the paper blank since he couldn't think of anything to write. The school director, my interpreter, responded, "Take some more time." I quietly moved toward Thomas and put my hand on his shoulder, praying for the Holy Spirit to guide him.

At the end of the group, Thomas told us he had been abandoned by the woman he loved the year before. He kept a chocolate wrapper in his Bible because she had taken a bite of the chocolate, and the wrapper had become an idol to him. When I put my hand on him, the Holy Spirit told him his wound wouldn't heal if he kept the wrapper. Thomas shares:

> I was in a valley of grief. God told me, "I want to take your wounds, but you don't want to give them to me. Get up and give the chocolate wrapper to the school leader." And the movement of the Holy Spirit was so great I could not live without doing it.

> Then God gave me complete healing from that wound. I have another wound, but over time God is healing me of that as well.

I recognized Thomas had a deep hunger for Jesus, for humble yet impactful ministry, and a desire to leave the earthly kingdom behind to pursue the heavenly one. I learned courage from him. It is not easy to be vulnerable, and to be obedient to what God asks instead of crippled by what people might think.

I returned to Islamabad and offered a two-day workshop for Christian women leaders. Conditions are extremely difficult for everyone in Pakistan, but particularly for women. They face unique challenges not only in cultural values but expectations for women, no matter their faith. When I hear their stories, I have a better understanding of real-life experiences instead of what is reported by the media.

I was particularly drawn to one of the women in the workshop, Julia. I sensed such spiritual and emotional maturity in her and asked her to return for a full week of training ten days later. Julia agreed. I learned she not only has experience as a human resource director but also has a bachelor's degree in psychology. Julia offers counseling in two schools and a hostel for both students and teachers, and provides individual, couple and group counseling. I look forward to having Julia join me as a co-facilitator when I return to Pakistan sometime in the future. Julia said:

> Many women who were in past trauma and grief never got out of it. They never take time to stay in the valley of weeping and just came out due to pressure of something. It helped them to go back and take rest in the valley of weeping so they can move on by the grace of God. They were strengthened, were being healed and could stand strong. I love working in a field where I can bind people and strengthen them because healed people can heal others.

The next week our small team drove off for Kashmir, land occupied by India (Hindu), China (Buddhist), and Pakistan (Muslim). I dressed in Pakistani clothes, kept my head covered, and sat farther back in the van. I wasn't afraid, but cautious and alert, aware of potential dangers.

I reflected on two experiences during my first visit to Pakistan. When I arrived for my connection at the Dubai airport, I noticed men and women sat separately. I studied their dress, their mannerisms, hoping to gain a better understanding of their culture. I could not blend in with blue eyes and blond hair. All eyes were on me when I entered the plane. The flight attendant asked, "Where are you from? And what are you going to do in Pakistan?"

I thought, *I wish you had not asked me that*, but answered, "I'm a psychologist from the US. I've been asked to provide training in mental health and trauma."

I sat down and tried to be invisible. The man sitting next to me talked constantly and loudly, so the people on the small plane continuously stared at me. He asked me questions; he shared his story and problems for three hours. He agonized over arranged marriages and conflicts between his wife and mother. He rarely gets home, which contributes to the problem.

"Are you Catholic or Orthodox?" He asked.

"I'm Christian," I answered.

He invited me to his village, saying his family was open-minded. Disembarking, he commented on my Pakistani clothes. I said, "Yes, that was my plan."

He said, "That's a good plan. Be careful."

This young Muslim man accompanied me to the baggage area, purposefully protecting me until I had my bags. And on every flight since, young men are seated next to me and tell me their life stories. I know it's not coincidental. God has placed me in this region for a specific purpose.

Then my thoughts returned to a pastor from Kashmir who had attended the DTS training I offered eight years earlier. He had guided me outside and pointed to a distant mountain range. "That's Pakistani Kashmir," he said. I had the sense that one day I would offer training in Kashmir and have continued to pray for Kashmir since that moment several years ago.

My thoughts returning to the present, our small team was on the way to Kashmir. The team manager received multiple phone calls, and we learned there were some concerns with the training. A five-day workshop was planned, but due to miscommunication we spent only one day in Kashmir.

While I was disappointed, I did have one day to pray for the land and the territories surrounding it. I had waited several years to step foot in Kashmir, and now I would soon be leaving. But the Holy Spirit whispered as I walked on the roof, "A day is as a thousand years." The pastor I had met years earlier came to see me and walked with me on the balcony.

"Look over there," he said. "That's Indian Kashmir. We ride our bikes and share the gospel." The persecuted church, at its tenacious best and with unswerving faith.

Another workshop was offered in Islamabad when the team returned. This group was extremely complicated since we had a mixture of church leaders from Kashmir, Afghan refugees, and Christians who fled Jaranwala after more than twenty churches and eighty homes were vandalized or destroyed. The incident in Jaranwala started because two Christians were falsely accused of blaspheming the Quran, which infuriated Muslims. A few people died and several were injured by a mob of over 5,000 people. To date, many people of Jaranwala experience discrimination and have unresolved trauma.

My head was spinning from the English, Urdu, Persian and Arabic languages all being spoken at the same time. And my heart was breaking from the horrendous stories of trauma. One woman's son was tortured and murdered by the Taliban, and her other son had been captured. Words comfort little, but human arms wrap wounded souls under the soothing wings of Jesus. Often, compassion is what's most needed. Each act of kindness leads people closer to the One who heals all wounds.

Our team went to the national monument and read the history of the four regions of Pakistan. We heard singing, and someone said, "Praise the Lord." As we returned from the monument, we heard, "Pray for Pakistan." The sounds of worship and prayer drew us near, and we found an open-air stadium with 3,500 people from

70 different churches worshiping together. Serving in missions provides spiritual experiences that carry me when I walk for miles in the wilderness.

The hotel had an inner courtyard where I could walk and pray each evening. I met several Afghan refugees waiting for visas to relocate in other countries, each with his or her own story. One young man had been persecuted by the Taliban for his gender choice. Anyone can experience persecution; it's not limited to people of different faith groups. I am so very thankful to live in a free country and am grateful I can share my faith openly. But those who know Jesus have an advantage no matter where we live. We have eternal hope. Those who don't know Him often suffer alone and in despair.

TILTI plans leadership projects in surrounding countries, and I hope mental health plays a small part in program development. South Asia and the Middle East are complicated regions, but nothing is impossible with God. My responsibility is to listen to His voice and obey when He speaks. Nothing more; nothing less.

Chapter Twenty-Three

Central Africa

Mercy Ships serves in different countries simultaneously since there are typically two ships providing life-changing care. The country engagement team builds relationships with both government ministries and church leaders prior to the ten-month field service. Both Cameroon and the Democratic Republic of the Congo (DRC) were countries designated by Mercy Ships for field service, which included mental health projects before and after.

Cameroon

Cameroon is a nation with two national languages—French and English. All the training workshops were held in the Francophone sectors due to civil conflict in other areas, and we experienced true partnership as we worked together for the nation. I asked Laure Menguene, the deputy director of mental health in Cameroon, if she wanted to facilitate the training. She said, "No! I want to learn." Not only did Laure attend the training, but she also offered to take part in some of our dramas and exercises. This is rare for a top-ranking psychiatrist in her field.

After the workshop, Laure developed and implemented a program for people with severe mental disorders who have no homes. Both populations are riddled with complexity, but Laure pours herself into their lives. She has met much resistance in developing the program, but her tenacity and selfless service bring healing to many. She named the program "Village of Love." Laure said the training has helped her explain mental health in simple words, sensitize the public, understand the difference between medical problems and spiritual ones, and the relationship between them. Laure shared the following story:

> I am managing cases holistically, which means physical, soul, spirit, and social relationships. I talk about spirituality because most patients are Christian. For example, when women are complaining about their child, I use psychotherapy and include the spiritual aspect. I ask them if they know where breath comes from. They often say, "My child, my child, they are sad." I understand. I tell them to know that Someone gives the ability to breathe; He also has His Word in our life, etc. Let us be humble and recognize, yes, it's our child, but Somebody else can decide for their life. When it's difficult, let's go to God and pray for the child because He is the one who gives life.
>
> I have learned so much about humility as a team and working together and hope to do the same in Cameroon. You are so close to the pupils, and with their reality. The training has helped me in my personal life, the way I interact with my children, my pupils, and God. May God bless you for all that you did for me with the training, and for all the people I successfully treat because of you.

Laure has become a dear friend over the years we have served together. Laure's smile, intellect, capacity, integrity, passion for people, and love for God inspire me to be better at everything I do.

Ministry can become overwhelming, and during those times I think I'm the only one on the battlefield. Elijah thought he was the only one standing against the prophets of Baal, but God reminded Elijah that 7,000 others had not bowed down to idols. The enemy wants us to believe the weight of the world is on our shoulders—no one else understands the responsibility. When I work alongside someone like Laure, I stand strong, knowing I am not alone.

A new team member, Georges, joined us in Cameroon during the spiritual leader training workshop. Georges is an organizer of the Cameroon National Prayer Breakfast, a master of internal book design and loves the field of mental health. He is a gifted interpreter and stepped in when a team member left for a family emergency. Georges willingly serves whenever he has time, and he does so with excellence. Amid difficulties, the team has learned God knows our needs and provides even before we ask.

Democratic Republic of the Congo (DRC)

Mercy Ships plans which country they will visit up to five years before a ship arrives, and mental health projects were part of the preparation phase. As a result, the mental health team might be the first Mercy Ships project in a country. This was the case for the Democratic Republic of the Congo. The DRC is the only country where the mental health team went pre-ship, and unforeseen circumstances made it impossible for a ship to follow.

The team has served twice in the DRC, a nation reeling from the effects of war for decades. One evening, the team sat by the Congo River and noticed Congo Brazzaville just across the water. How sad—another land divided with no way to travel back and forth. Families separated; a culture unable to connect. Currently, the DRC has many theaters of war orchestrated by M23 rebel groups, among others. We maintain contact with our partners in the area of conflict and displacement in the north.

After training three separate groups of church leaders, social workers, and health care workers, we planned a networking session at the end of the last day. The participants were segregated by service provider group, but the room filled with energy as participants shared how changes in their approach brought more people for counseling. Dividing walls began to fall as participants recognized these diverse provider groups now had a common perspective on mental health. Participants shared phone numbers with each other at the end of the gathering. This is our intention. To see service providers empower, encourage, collaborate, and hold each other accountable regarding what they learn.

A year later, the team arranged a Zoom meeting for participants to reconnect and hear challenges and success stories. We learned that participants across service provider groups had partnered to use *Baby Finds Grace* with 40,000 children living in the far north who had fled from rebel groups. This, like many other success stories, would not be known without follow-up.

Years later I traveled to the DRC for Tributaries and worked in a conflict-riddled region in the north. A ministry named Elikia had been using *Baby Finds Grace* with children, and the team returned to give them additional training in *Understanding People, Mental Health and Trauma*. I was moved as I watched the children express through drama how *Baby Finds Grace* made a difference in their lives.

Eddy, a gifted and compassionate leader, shared the story of a young girl who had experienced significant trauma due to sexual assault. At first, she was withdrawn, but over time she developed trust and started to share her experiences. Eddy wrote:

> One day, during an art session, she created a painting that depicted her journey from darkness to light. This breakthrough moment not only revealed her healing but also inspired other children in the program. She has since become an advocate for children facing similar challenges.

After visiting with the children, I was taken to a separate home where Elikia houses young women who have experienced sexual assault. The women dramatized a traumatic event that occurred while gathering wood in isolated areas. In the drama, they graphically demonstrated being overpowered, but more importantly, how Elikia joins them in the healing journey. The drama was sobering and heart-wrenching, but I was struck by how much healing had already occurred for these women to be so vulnerable in the drama.

Delphine, Elikia's director, is dedicated, inspirational, and capable. He shared the following story from one of the young women who participated in the gripping drama.

> Two of my friends and I went to the woods looking for firewood. It was the middle of the day. Two men in military uniform and a weapon forced themselves on us. We refused and fled. My two friends succeeded to escape but I did not. A mother far away in her field heard the screams so she left quickly to call other men to help me. When the aggressor heard there were people coming to help, he quickly ran away and left me there. They took me to the hospital for treatment. I couldn't do any activities, and I was scared and cry a lot when I remember the event. I still don't know what happened to my friends.
>
> I followed the *Baby Finds Grace* manual, and it helped me a lot. Baby's story is really my life. Today I feel I am a winner over shame and fears. Thank you very much to Elikia who was a parent to me, and God, and *Baby Finds Grace*, I'm saved. I find that I will be a woman of value in this world. I will continue my studies and thank you for the Bible. God bless you, Elikia, for everything.

Delphine told me the team prays for me every day, and missionaries have no doubt we are dependent on prayer. During ongoing conflict and trauma, Elikia prays for others. Only God knows the impact they make. I too, say, *Thank you, Elikia, for your prayers and your faithful service.*

I heard a bird singing outside the window one morning while eating breakfast. I asked another guest, "Is that a grey parrot?"

"Yes," she said. "He comes here often and hangs around the kitchen. You might be able to see him if you go now." I'd never seen a grey parrot during any of my trips to Central Africa, and it is a central character in *Baby Finds Grace*. Anticipating success but prepared for disappointment, I hurried to the yard. There he was, sitting on the fence, singing to connect with his friend in the kitchen.

The cook came out, and the grey parrot climbed onto his hand, just like Baby on Pierre's hand, on the cover of *Baby Finds Grace*. I watched; I waited. The cook asked, "Would you like to touch him?" Of course, I did. I nodded, then reached out to touch the beautiful creation in front of me. His song triggered sweet memories of Grace inviting me in with her words, "Hello! Welcome!"

After a minute or so, I looked over to see the resident guard dog watching us, with a desperate desire for human touch and compassion. He looked so lonely. After the cook left, I walked slowly to the dog, wanting to ease his sorrowful soul. He lay on his side, and I stroked his belly. His tail wagged. I then massaged his back, and he looked at me with what appeared to be a smile. He made sounds like a deep moan, still with his tail wagging.

A few seconds later, I touched his head. Instinctively, he bit my hand, then recoiled. *Too late now*, I thought. *I might get rabies.* It wasn't his fault; I misread his behavior. What I thought was pleasure was a defensive maneuver. The smile was to show his teeth, and though he wagged his tail, his groan was fear.

I did not touch the dog again until the last day, aware he likely experienced abusive head trauma (ABT) in the past. I waited outside for Eddy and Delphine to take me to the airport, but when they arrived, the dog charged and growled at them. When the dog noticed I was walking with them, he hesitated, then stood beside me as if to apologize. I bent down low to pet him, deliberately avoiding his head. It seemed as if the dog knew I cared and was not angry with him. We do this with people, too. We approach without knowing the story and are surprised by the response.

Kay and I have served and traveled together for many years. She has become one of my closest friends, and she brings a mixture of gifts desperately needed to develop and maintain an effective ministry. Kay is one of the most intelligent and creative people I know, with a huge heart for God and for missions.

Mental health training is unique since every day offers opportunities to grow. It is not like teaching a mathematics course, which, though valuable, does not add to healthy life and relationships. Participants think they are coming for training to help others. But in the process, all of us change in a positive way if we are willing to do so. Kay shares stories of how mental health training has impacted her.

> After the training I am more understanding and patient, and more comfortable talking about emotions. I now consider another person's life experiences rather than being quick to judge, and I believe I have become a better person.
>
> I'm also better equipped for intervening in life-threatening situations. One day, a very upset man acted strangely in my front yard. It seemed like he might become violent, throwing his bicycle, yelling, and throwing his phone on the ground. I approached him calmly and breathed slowly; he also calmed, and we talked. I wondered if he thought of harming himself. I was able to ask him directly, and he told me he had been sitting by the water all night thinking about jumping in but had decided to go home. He was still very angry with himself. His phone kept ringing, so I asked him who was calling and if people were worried about him. He showed me the texts of people asking where he was and if he was okay. I told him he had people who seemed to care a lot about him, and I asked him where he would go. He told me he would

> go to one of his friends who was texting him. Eventually he went on his way, talking to one of those people on the phone. I would not have attempted that conversation without the training.

The way Kay responded to the man in her story is a much more appropriate response than my response to the lonely dog. Understanding people (and all creatures great and small) is a lifelong process.

Chapter Twenty-Four

Liberia

The Mercy Ships mental health team returned to Liberia in November 2022. While in the country, I received news that the Mental Health Program would be discontinued after our final project in Senegal in 2023. The program was often in jeopardy since the primary mission of Mercy Ships is life-changing surgeries. I wasn't surprised by the decision, but I grieved. I reflected on where I had been and how God would move me forward.

Liberia had only one psychiatrist when the Mental Health Program began in 2007. More than eighteen years later, there is still only one, though others are being trained. With a population of over five million people, those plagued with mental disorders or trauma have few resources available. Resources increase through our training of primary health care workers, including physicians of several specialties, and informal service providers such as spiritual leaders. I have heard both painful and heartwarming stories over the years. Here are just a few.

The tribe that chose Joshua as high priest more than forty years ago, now chooses to follow Jesus. Nya-bwe-a-weh, the demon they served, has less influence, and the land has been set free by the Spirit of God. While some people continue to worship Nya-bwe-a-weh secretly, much of the tribe are Jesus followers. Originally the elders tried to kill Joshua when he became a Christian, because it was forbidden to choose a new high priest while the current high priest remained alive. Since they have turned to Jesus, the tribe flourishes.

The mental health team offered a project in Sinoe County, the region of Nya-bwe-a-weh's seat of power. Four of us walked through the jungle to locate the rock he claims as his home. How sad. A massive rock, created by God but desecrated by demonic powers. I solemnly considered how idols of stone, wood, and clay enslave people desperate for guidance and power from something inanimate. The book of Isaiah speaks often of how senseless it is to trust in idols, and the prophet pleads with people to seek God. "I am", says the Lord, "I always was."

I prayed at the rock, and I claimed that everywhere I put my feet was holy ground. Jesus lives in me. He will not share His glory with anyone. I visited with Joshua when I returned to Monrovia, and when I shared my experience at the rock, he said, "You could only get close to the rock because Nya-bwe-a-weh has lost his power."

I countered, "He may have lost influence, but he has not lost his power. Demons continue to roam the earth, seeking whom they may devour. I could stand by the rock and pray because Jesus in me is greater than he who is in the world. Demons cower in the presence of Jesus. The stone fortress, at most, is merely a rock."

Just as I prayed for increased territory for Jesus, I pray my investment through mental health training and my personal relationship with Joshua plays some small part in this supernatural shift. Dramatic manifestations where Jesus conquers, and demonic powers fall, factualizes that prayer and ministry impact the spiritual realm for good.

Joshua and his children founded Journey Against Violence (JAV), an organization to house young people who were living on the streets and addicted to drugs. Some of these youths are under ten years old, with tragic stories of childhood trauma. Joshua provides a safe place for them not only to heal but to meet Jesus as their personal Savior and loving Father. Currently, there are approximately 110 boys and ten girls being set free from drugs, homelessness, and trauma.

Moses is a health care worker, and I worked in his clinic in 2007. Moses has a huge heart, develops lasting friendships, and has just opened a new organization named Global Relief Action for Social Protection (GRASP). Together, we had found a school for Jane, the deaf and mute child, where she could heal from trauma and develop skills to thrive.

Jane has now graduated and guides other special needs children at this amazing school. Jane continues with education and has learned she has a God-given purpose regardless of her limitations. The mother gave me a graduation photo of Jane, a reminder that taking action matters. I am so thankful Jesus looks for the one.

Sorsor is a church leader who has lifted my arms during each project in Liberia since 2008. I could depend on Sorsor to accompany me to remote areas, make sardine sandwiches in the back of the room as I facilitated training in the front, and locate past participants and ministry partners. I reconnect to maintain meaningful relationships and also to learn how the mental health training impacts kingdom growth. Sorsor reconnected me with Oscar.

In 2008, the mental health team offered a training for Great Commission, an organization founded by Campus Crusade. Anastas, the director of Great Commission, connected seventeen churches for the purpose of "Turning Crime Spots into Calm Spots." Oscar, the gang leader and doorkeeper of Sugar Hill, began his Christian journey soon after.

Oscar is now Pastor Moses, a name given by a group of missionaries who said he was called to lead others out of the ghettos. Moses is the founder of the ministry Fishers of Men, and his first outreach was bringing a crusade to Sugar Hill. Church leaders from our training in 2008 joined him there. Oscar's team continues outreach to street boys and girls who are hooked on drugs, and he has pastored a church for over ten years.

Sugar Hill is no longer impenetrable. In fact, young people I spoke to recently did not know Sugar Hill existed. These stories demonstrate the amazing love and power of God and simultaneously encourage our team to continue when we face challenges.

I met Ben in 2008 and recognized immediately that he loved Jesus and loved people. Ben is a pensive person, who diligently served as principal of a Christian school. In 2018 I phoned Ben because the caterer for a new training group was unavailable, and I needed to locate one within two days. Ben said he knew one and would also provide the venue to initiate *Baby Finds Grace* with children. When I told Ben what we could pay for the caterer, he replied, "No, that's too much." Ben recently shared some of his journey with me.

> I was going through emotional challenges when I met Lyn. My attempts at getting married had failed, and I started to develop a negative self-concept. Lyn asked me, "Ben, what if you set other goals and release your energy if marriage is not working?" I felt like someone lifted a burden off my shoulders. My interaction with Lyn helped me develop different frameworks or lenses for navigating life.
>
> Some of the comments that have resonated with me over the years include, "People are complex." "Things that can be a bump in the road for some people, for others, it could be a mountain." "Effective people try to understand people rather than to be understood." I am happily married, have three wonderful kids, and Charlene and I do what we do because seventeen years ago, I met someone who took an interest in me and helped me see the brighter side of life.

Ben and his wife Charlene work with couples, in family enrichment, educating future teachers in assessing and serving children, in addition to serving the large church he founded. They also work with children who live in less privileged homes, including city jungles and slums. Ben is currently completing a doctorate in ministry. I continue to be amazed by his humility, integrity, and generosity. He reminds me it is more blessed to give than to receive.

The combination of history, cultural practices, different tribes, and languages creates complexities not explained with simple responses. Conflicts occur within countries and between countries over many issues.

One of these conflicts is faith. It plays a critical part in the lives of many people, and yet conflicts may occur because of faith preferences. Liberia is primarily a Christian nation with both Protestants and Catholics, but there are also animists and Muslims. I often see a separation between Protestants and Catholics and hope my small contribution toward connecting the different groups precipitates change. One way I do this is integrating participants from different faith groups. During the training, I intentionally have people sit next to people of different faiths instead of gathering with their friends.

I met Martin in Monrovia during the Fall of 2019, when he requested training at the seminary. I was impressed by his effort, humility, gentleness and sensitivity to the needs of others. Martin has advanced degrees and serves as administrator at the Sacred Heart Cathedral, as an educator at the University of Liberia, and writes and administers diocese policy for the Child Protection Commission of the Catholic Church.

During the training, Martin shared his experience and loss in the civil war when he was sixteen years old. He suffered trauma during a three-day crisis event in which his family was on the move to save their lives. It was unexpected, because the belief had been that the "freedom fighters" would not harm ordinary people. Terrified, the family traveled deserted streets, with the sound of guns pounding the air. They stayed overnight with friends, but the next morning rebels found them and made them leave with nothing except the clothes they were wearing. His father was stopped at a security checkpoint, arrested, and taken away. That was the last day my friend saw his father, and what is most difficult for him and his siblings is that there is no physical place to remember their father. I was moved by Martin's current reflection on the painful story from his childhood.

> I sometimes hope he is alive somewhere in the world. Other times, I say to him, papa, we are all alive; the war did not kill us; the children you gave your life for. Thank you for treating us special. I love you—an expression in his lifetime he never got to hear from me. I treasured those moments with him on the soccer field; those times he appreciated me with gifts on my birthday. My father is my hero. He lived as a quiet and peaceful man, honest, with love for people—especially his children. He also taught us to be independent, and to follow the rule of law. The civil crisis changed my life, and the life of my siblings, in a hard way. But I am far better than years ago. I recognize God can bring good from evil. My father would want me to work peacefully and unassumingly rather than approach life with hate, anger, and distress. I learned to not only get in touch with my story but also, I try to accept it. I want to look at the glass-half-full side of my story.

It's so easy to say I see the glass half full but not as easy to do it. Martin models that for me. Thank you, Martin, for your service to Liberia, especially protection of children.

I met Ibnyasin, a mental health clinician, during a training in Liberia in 2019. He works in government service, including providing mental health care for inmates at Monrovia Central Prison. He is devoted to Jesus, to those suffering from mental disorders, and to his family. No challenge is too large for him. I was drawn to him during our training because he was attentive to content, but also passionate about serving disadvantaged populations with excellence. Ibnyasin shared:

> After acquiring knowledge as a mental health clinician, my love and feelings for people with mental disorders has grown and I want them to be loved and cared for as all human beings should be treated. I also want them to be valued by society. I used the Behavior Process Model and anger management from the training with a particular inmate, and he is now doing so well he was granted early release. Every time he sees me on the street he runs to me, and tells people that God and Ibnyasin, in that order, have had a positive impact on his life.

I could write an entire book about my life, experiences, and relationships in Liberia after the many visits I have had and it being the country of the first mental health project. Serving in foreign missions is bittersweet. Mobile long-term missionaries love sharing Jesus but grieve the loss of relationships moving from country to country. Jesus created us for relationship; we count the cost and are grateful for the privilege.

Chapter Twenty-Five

West Africa

I've spent much time on the continent of Africa for the better part of two decades. Mercy Ships predominantly serves in West Africa, and both Tributaries and SEAPC have added projects there through requests from ministry partners and long-term team members.

Some of the countries are Anglophone, while others are Francophone. I've become fluid in moving among them. However, I do so wish I had the gift of language and could interact more freely with colleagues and participants. This chapter includes stories from Togo, Senegal, and Côte d'Ivoire.

Togo

Togo is a small and widely diverse country, but what I love most is that two of my long-term team members are Togolese. Mercy Ships and Tributaries have both offered projects in Togo.

The mental health team starts a children's workshop whenever possible during our projects. This gives the leaders experience with children and gives our team an opportunity to ensure the groups are led with skill and compassion. One story gives a glimpse of incredible love in action.

Mama Charity and her team attended a training for orphanage workers because they were struggling and discouraged by children experiencing trauma with behavioral issues. During follow-up, Charity said the home was calmer, and stress management techniques helped them develop new strategies to work with the children. Charity said:

> I'm not a psychologist by profession, but I realized I am playing the role of a counselor. Many girls are abandoned with babies. Everyone runs to the orphanage, crying, "Mama, Mama—my husband has run away, and I have this baby. Help me!" Now I'm calm. I listen. I calm them, and we try to find solutions.

Most children in orphanages are there because the parents struggle to provide the most basic needs—not because there isn't a family. Charity counsels the mothers and helps them realize their own worth. She identifies skills, encourages them, and helps them find or create work. She now keeps over 300 children during the day so their mothers can work.

Charity knows the pain of losing a child. She lost her three children to illness while they were still small. She has experienced much grief but finds healing in loving the children around her.

I narrowly escaped losing my son to cancer and nearly relapsed into depression. Charity lost three children yet opened her home to many children and mothers. Her bright smile, her tenderness, demonstrate the nature and character of a loving God. I hope I've learned from Charity how to genuinely embrace the pain of watching loved ones suffer while powerless in the natural to help.

Two Togolese team members, Samuel and Soulé, have served alongside me (and sometimes without me) since 2010. We are like family. We can anticipate potential issues and strengthen each other when tragedies in any of our lives occur. They both have countless stories to tell of changes in their own lives, and in those they love and serve.

Samuel is a master of Scripture and a lifelong learner. His quiet demeanor and ability to be "slow to speak" provide a cushion from external stressors for our team. I never doubt Samuel's love for Jesus, mental health and wholeness, and discipleship. He received healing from multiple losses and extended forgiveness to others. Samuel holds bachelor, master, and doctoral degrees from divinity schools, and is an ordained minister. His Bible college has now become a university, and he is founding a wellness center.

Samuel shares:

> I travelled with a *New York Times* journalist to visit prayer centers. He wanted to write about how people suffering from mental disorders are treated and on the use of chains. I suggested types of restraints other than chains, and informed prayer camp leaders of the need to consider other areas of the whole person. I also recommended medical check-ups and lab tests for people presenting symptoms of "demon possession" to see if their problems may be medical. Two prayer centers created a health post on their premises. I contacted one of them this year, and the health center is still operational with a permanent nurse. They now do referrals.
>
> Today, mental health has become part of my life. The Westman Framework is present in all my activities. The question "Why do people do what they do?" is always considered when a matter

concerning behavior is put before me. I continue to regard Lyn as my mentor.

Soulé also serves as a facilitator, interpreter, and translator for mental health. He easily connects with others, reads psychological and medical textbooks for fun, and is himself an open book. His yes is yes, and his no is no. Soulé is a man of prayer and worship; he is an ordained minister. His favorite saying is, "Everything in Africa needs prayer, discipline, and proactivity." Soulé has a broader calling to the global church and is an encourager to everyone he meets.

Soulé had been deeply wounded by a previous mentor and was harboring unforgiveness. The workshop gave him time to heal and gain new hope and strength to continue in ministry. He told me he had learned to put God first, family second, and ministry third.

Soulé shared mental health content with his wife, who was able to grieve, heal, and forgive, and he taught his good friend, a surgeon who was having marital concerns. The couple reconciled, and together Soulé and the surgeon offered workshops in the local area with medical personnel, teachers, imams, traditional healers, and church leaders. They built a referral network to offer care from a holistic perspective.

Follow-up with health care workers provided many success stories. For example, the national mental health coordinator developed a master's level nursing program, which has trained forty-nine students. And mental health professionals organized an active mental health association in Lomé and in six different regions of Togo. Participants from all provider groups join, which strengthens the organization. We are inspired by the creativity and dedication of the mental health professionals to increase the capacity and availability of care for clients.

Senegal

The mental health team offered the first Mercy Ships project since 1993 in Senegal. An estimated 92 percent of the population of Senegal is Muslim, and many Christians experience persecution. Church leader participants from the first week of training effectively facilitated the training with a later group.

Waly Saar was the president of Assemblies of God in Senegal until 2023. Currently, he serves as the director of the Assemblies of God Biblical and Theological Institute. I love when people in positions of power become pupils with the rest of their teams. At the end of the mental health training, Waly said, "The training was timely, giving us another avenue of ministry to serve the Church. When people suffered and exhibited strange behavior in the past, church leaders cast out demons, which left the suffering person in no better—or perhaps worse—condition."

Waly recently shared an update:

> We've been doing both counseling and deliverance since the training. Before doing deliverance, we learn the background of the person by listening to him/her or inquiring from those who know him/her to decide what to do. If deliverance is necessary, we do that but follow it up with counseling. In case it doesn't necessitate deliverance, we carry on with counseling.
>
> We once did deliverance for a girl in the church for many hours during an all-night prayer to no avail. She went through counseling after and baptism class; today she is a Sunday school teacher.

Deliverance is a process. The person's story needs to be considered before deciding on an approach. Deliverance may be immediate, or it may take time. Counseling is deliverance, but the change occurs slowly. Less darkness leads to more light. Less pain leads to more peace.

Amid purpose, personal struggles ensue. Soon after the initial Senegal project, the COVID-19 pandemic disrupted my life in countless ways. I was in West Africa when Covid became a global issue, and plans changed by the minute. I was scheduled for a three-day trip to offer a short project in another country, but I received a message from Mercy Ships as soon as I landed, saying that I might need to leave immediately.

It was stifling hot in my room, and mosquitoes were active. I had no cell phone service in this remote location, which made receiving updates difficult. I quickly compressed content, but was also told to offer the training in both English and French. I then needed to make the two-hour drive to the airport after training to catch a night flight back to the US.

Every in-person project was cancelled. This meant I needed to provide training using technology, which is my nemesis. Not only am I technically challenged, but I believe mental health training is best achieved through face-to-face interaction. Technology caused even more stress for me than overseas travel and harsh living conditions.

I contracted Covid in May of 2022, while serving again in Senegal. By Saturday of the first week, I had an excruciating headache and a fever of 103. Living in a hotel provided no access to health care, and for an entire ten days I was too sick to get out of bed. After another five days, I was able to go to the celebration dinner with our team and chose to dance to African music—determined Covid would not spoil my last evening before traveling back to the US I was grateful to have escaped Covid until Senegal but afterward I experienced how life-altering it is. I continue to suffer from the effects of long Covid and complications from multiple vaccines.

The final year in Senegal, we offered a workshop for a mixed group of spiritual leaders. Some were Christian; some Muslim; some traditional; and some humanists. I taught about spiritual counseling the final day and was drawn to a young man seated on the first row. I shared the Scripture from Hosea 11 that says when we were children, God loved us. But the more He loved us, the further we went away, sacrificing to the Baals. It reads,

> "It was I who taught Ephraim to walk, taking them by the arms; but they did not realize it was I who healed them. I led them with cords of human kindness, with ties of love. To them I was like one who lifts a little child to the cheek, and I bent down to feed them. (Hosea 11:3-4)"

As I spoke these words, I moved toward Bassirou, looked into his eyes, and bent down in front of him.

At the closing ceremony, Bassirou asked if he could speak. He said, "I used to think God was so far away. Now I feel Him so close." I connected him with a pastor to disciple him. Recently, a team member called Bassirou, who said, "The training has helped me so much on many things spiritually. Because after the training I went to get a Bible which I keep reading. This has enabled me to understand the Christian religion and to glorify the Lord Jesus, son of God."

Bassirou remains a Muslim but draws near to God. Those who seek Him will find Him.

Côte d'Ivoire

I agreed to mentor a missionary for two years, who was moving to Abengourou with her family of five. We further collaborated to plan a mental health workshop, and participants included clinic staff and church leaders from within their denomination. One pastor, Chris, shared with participants that he had done many terrible things in his past, and had been detained by the authorities. He described horrific conditions, cramped space, and many unmet needs during detention. Chris met with me privately to share his trauma and how it affected him.

> My father was a pastor and extremely harsh in discipline, which created deep wounds in me and a gap between us. I had some character crises which led me into a deadly cult called Sons of Darkness. After initiation, my world was suddenly filled with darkness. I began to sense a violent spirit moving over me like a wave, taking control of me, and I lost all compassion and kindness. I was armed with destructive weapons and poisonous powders and was prepared to use them when needed. Though I was climbing the ladder, I was insecure and feared my enemies. Drugs became my comfort and courage. Over a ten-year period, I was constantly in trouble with the law.
>
> By 1997, I realized my future only held death and hell, but how could I escape since I had sworn a lifelong oath? I cried out to the God I had ignored for ten years to save me.
>
> God heard me and made way for my deliverance by opening the door to Côte d'Ivoire. I went to several churches but then heard a message just for me at the Evangelical Church of God, and I was reborn as a new person. I have switched from the Sons of Darkness to the Sons of Light.
>
> I became aware of many things during the training. Because my father treated me so badly, I have treated my daughter like a father should—with love, kindness, respect, and encouragement. But I now realize I have not treated my wife with the same respect. When I return home, I will treat my wife better.

Thank you, Chris, for your vulnerability and willingness to tell your story. God's redemptive message is revealed through testimonies shared with humility.

We visited the Basilica of Our Lady of Peace in Yamoussoukro. The structure is massive, strikingly beautiful with marble from Italy and stained-glass windows from France. I find peace as I move softly through Christian sanctuaries, drawn in by the stained glass. I know God is with me as I walk. The tour guide shared the mysteries and history of this magnificent site and stopped to explain the stories of the statues surrounding us.

One statue depicted Joseph, the natural father of Jesus, as he worked as a carpenter. The tour guide pointed out that Jesus was looking at Joseph because, as God, he already knew how to do carpentry. He didn't need to learn by watching his father. The statue struck me differently. I saw Jesus, looking intently into the eyes of his father Joseph because he cares more about relationships than our craft. I imagine Him looking at me in the same way—as His dearly beloved daughter.

Chapter Twenty-Six

Southern Africa

I have offered mental health training in several countries in Southern Africa, but only South Africa and Zambia are included here. The partnerships were formed either through Mercy Ships or through SEAPC.

South Africa

I never tire of returning to South Africa with its delicious blend of natural beauty, culture, people, and my favorite food, lamb chops. The two primary dialects are Xhosa and Zulu, though many people speak Afrikaans and/or English. In some ways, South Africa reminds me of Chicago with its racial and cultural diversity and the striking differences among its regions. I feel at home in South Africa. Mercy Ships has offered multiple projects in various parts of the country, both Zulu and Xhosa, including children's workshops. All the South Africa stories include people who have had training and provide counseling or build capacity in their nations.

Naomi, from Cape Town, has been a team member with me since 2008. I love her laugh, her sense of humor, her insight, and her compassion for wounded people. But personally, I can rely on her to follow through on everything she commits to with excellence and integrity. Naomi has a spiritual gift of counseling but has also pursued education and blends the two beautifully. Naomi and I have become fast friends over the years, and she shares her story with us.

> The Mental Health Program has changed my perception of mental disorders. Before the program I stigmatized people with

> mental disorders, but now I understand people and have more compassion toward them. I see people differently because I've learned people are complex.
>
> When I attended the mental health training in 2008, I was inspired to do my bachelor's degree in theology with biblical counseling as my major. My husband and I started Sowing Seeds of Joy South Africa in 2016, a ministry registered with the government of South Africa. I use the training with various groups of people, as well as train-the-trainer workshops which led to a few churches starting substance support groups and compassionate ministries in their churches. In addition, I counsel individuals and couples.
>
> I realize mental health has a great impact on our lives daily. Therefore, I believe if more people are aware of how important their mental health is, it will lead to positive holistic changes in their lives. When more mental health workshops are conducted, more people understand common mental disorders and how to deal with them. It's equally important for them to understand themselves and others.
>
> I counseled with an 8-year-old girl who told me she had anger issues. She said her anger is as big as the five balls I have in my office. Every week she would tell me her anger is getting less and less. When I asked her why her anger is getting less, she said, "You taught me what to do when I get angry and to tell people how I feel when I am unhappy."

Naomi is honest and straightforward. This is refreshing for me, because some people hide their true thoughts and feelings to avoid conflict or shame. Eventually, relationships are affected because when the truth is revealed, distance is created by both the conflict and the lack of honesty. I trust Naomi, which decreases my stress tremendously.

Christy joined the mental health team to co-facilitate a workshop with children who lived in the townships of Cape Town. The workshop was extremely complicated due to the level of violence the children experienced in the environment and now exhibited in their own behavior. Christy's gentle spirit and gift of encouragement calmed the children and added tremendously to the strength of our team. Christy is also an ordained minister, but I believe it is a well-kept secret. I'm encouraged when I watch people mature and live out their God-given purpose, knowing my life touched theirs in some small way. Christy shares stories from her time in South Africa.

I vividly remember the first day we started our small groups. The children had significant behavioral issues, including fighting, and had a difficult time adjusting to telling their stories in a group setting.

A 6-year-old boy shared about living with his single-parent mother. His uncle had allowed him and his mother to set up their home, a metal roof attached to the uncle's home in the slums. It was covered with a tarp and open to the elements. His mother got sick, most likely with TB, and she told him she was dying and there was nothing he could do. He told us he would go days without food just to share what little food they did have and would tell her he wasn't hungry just to make sure his mother had food. He spoke so kindly of her and then said when she died, he had no one and nothing, and his uncle couldn't care for him anymore. He was left on the streets until he was put into a children's home and then a foster care home.

When the boy shared his story, the other children sat quietly looking at their hands. It seems they understood no one should have to suffer this kind of pain. The dynamics of our group changed, and other children began to share their stories.

The boy later confided that this was the first time he had felt warmth and love since his mother had died two years before. He told us he felt unwanted and alone and had been isolated because he was an orphan. He prayed with members of the team at the end of the week to give his life to Christ, who would never leave him or forsake him because he was wanted and loved by God.

One of the last activities we did in our class was to draw a picture of something, and this boy drew a picture of a home that had walls and was warm. He wanted me to have it. He couldn't write his name, so I asked him to draw a picture of himself for me. He is giving himself a hug and is happy.

I am so grateful we co-facilitated with local South Africans who would continue to counsel and get the appropriate help for the children. They earned trust with the children during the week and would be able to connect the children with church organizations and mental health resources to continue the healing process.

Serving these children has forever changed how I provide mental healthcare for children, especially those who have experienced trauma at a particularly young age.

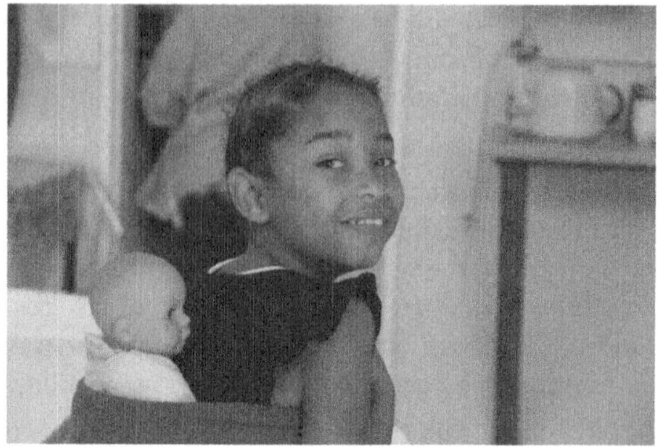

Zambia

I met a pastor named Alfred through SEAPC, and together we organized a mental health training workshop to be offered in Zambia. The nation is peaceful, predominantly Christian, and provides a greater level of spiritual calm than many countries where I serve. The team offered a workshop in Choma, a few hours' drive from the Zimbabwe border. Alfred and his wife Tessah hosted the training, and Tessah shared her story with me.

> My sister and I take care of our mother who is struggling with dementia. Before the mental health team came to offer training, we thought our mother had been bewitched by some people in our village. The hospital just told us to say this is old age. But we were puzzled by her strange behavior, because we had never heard of dementia. Some family members started suspecting other people to say they are the ones who are bewitching mom, and there was hatred in the family. I encouraged my brothers and sisters saying since we are Christians, let us continue trusting God and he will reveal everything to us.
>
> Lyn started teaching and explained about how a person with dementia behaves, and we realized that was exactly what Mom was struggling with. My sister and I talked with Lyn after the church service that our mother has this problem, so how can we take care of her? She advised us to show her love by listening to her, trying to understand her, and by building a supportive structure for her to create a safe environment and make her comfortable.
>
> After we learned about mental health, we started caring for her, understanding her and always making sure there is someone with her. Our attitude toward her condition has changed, and there is

peace in the family. The training has changed our perspective and empowered us to manage the situation.

Merilyn is the education, training, and administrative assistant on the *Global Mercy*, and has served as a facilitator with the mental health team since 2022 when we offered workshops in Senegal. Merilyn is perceptive, circumspect, wise, and compassionate. Merilyn hopes to begin a certification program in counseling. She already has a five-year bachelor's degree in psychology. Merilyn shares how the mental health training impacts her both professionally and personally.

> Joining the mental health team was a win-win for me. I have a background in psychology, and it gave me opportunity to be a part of work I am passionate about, while learning so much about understanding people and myself. I learned to speak and present with confidence on several topics found in the Westman Framework and am grateful for the opportunity to have traveled to different countries with her team. It was a special joy to join the team in Zambia, as I was born in Zambia.
>
> The most rewarding yield from these experiences was being empowered to facilitate several sessions using my favorite model, the Johari Window. I have had the privilege of facilitating sessions with the young women of my church at an annual retreat. I shared about how God has called us to live a transparent life, and the more transparent we are, the happier and freer we become.
>
> I have seen the truth of this in my own life, so it is only natural that I share it with others. Living a more transparent life involves allowing oneself to be sharpened by others who move elements out of the blind spot into the arena; being open about oneself by bringing things out of the façade into the arena; and by allowing God, in His perfect timing, to bring hidden hurts to light to make space for healing.
>
> I recently also facilitated a session with my team at work. We looked at how the Johari window can help us understand ourselves and each other better. We ended the session by encouraging each other, bringing things out of the blind spot into the arena. The blind spot not only includes negative things we don't know about ourselves, but it also includes positives we aren't aware of. We may not realize how our work is positively impacting those around us. It is encouraging when team members point these strengths out and bring them to light. We recognized each other's strengths and affirmed them. I am looking forward to facilitating more team-building sessions through the knowledge gained working with Lyn. I can attest to the power of living an authentic life.

> Working alongside Lyn allowed me to see that this is a healthy way to live.

Lions are my favorite animals, even more than bears. Some years ago, I learned it was possible to feed a bear at the Lions, Tigers & Bears Sanctuary in California. As I looked at the website, I realized I could also feed a lion named Bakari (One with Great Promise). *What? Why would I choose a bear when I can feed a lion?*

Bakari formidably charged toward me as I approached the cage. This majestic creature stood up, towering over me with such a powerful presence I was mesmerized. This momentary pause irritated Bakari, and he pounded his paw on the bars. His paw was larger than my head, and his demand for food jarred me back to reality. Bakari insisted on being fed, and I complied by sliding the meat-loaded stick through the thick iron bars. I was not afraid—I was in awe. Lions remind me of Jesus, the Lion of Judah, who became the sacrificial lamb to purchase our freedom.

I spent time with lions during my stay in Zambia. I didn't intend to go on the excursion because I was concerned that they might be treated poorly. In some parts of the world, animals are exploited, starved and mistreated instead of rescued. But a pastor told me these lions are bred to increase the population, and after three years they are released into the wild. They are well fed, but if they see a gazelle or other animal, the lions are free to chase the animals to preserve their predator instinct to survive when released.

Two lions, a male and a female approached, accompanied by eight men who fed and raised these incredible animals. My instructions were to stay behind or to the side, rather than in front of them so they wouldn't playfully jump on me and maul my face with their giant, Bakari-like paws. I could pet them, but with force. A gentle touch would trigger them to swat me with their tail, thinking I was a fly. I was the only tourist during my forty-five- minute walk with the lions, and the pleasure I experienced is indescribable. I thank God for the adventures He gives me and believe immersing myself in His creation brings a smile to His face.

Chapter Twenty-Seven

East Africa

Projects in East Africa were developed through established relationships with SIL, Wycliffe, Tributaries, and SEAPC, as well as through my church. SEAPC's prayer conferences created opportunities for cross-cultural connections with leaders from many nations. This chapter will focus on the work that was done in Uganda and Burundi.

Uganda

I have traveled to Uganda for different projects, beginning in 2008. The first trip was to the north in Gulu, where Joseph Kony led the Lord's Resistance Army (LRA), creating a reign of terror and leaving many children orphaned. The country was still volatile and war-torn. I joined SIL and Wycliffe to pilot the first children's trauma healing workshop, using the book *Bringing Healing to Children*, which I coauthored. Two young boys from different regions of Uganda wrote laments. The first wrote:

> Oh God, I called upon you because of this war in Northern Uganda. Listen to our prayers so that, if possible, the peace process going on in Juba can be fruitful. And Lord, I ask you for the problems we have experienced in Northern Uganda to be calm. Oh God, I called on you because of problems we are faced with. Thank you for saving me from the sin of anger that leads us to do evil.

I am struck by the level of understanding young children have into the motivations, the behaviors, and the outcomes that affect their lives. This young boy recognized that anger may lead to evil, and knows God is the one who can save him from sin. He also prayed for the peace process to be successful. Children are often expected to be seen and not heard, yet their wisdom and their prayers are powerful.

The second boy wrote:

> Dear God, I want to inform you that I have a problem with my aunt. My aunt does not want me to stay with her. But God, what can I do? She wants me to get where I can stay, but I don't have anyone to stay with. I would have gone to my mother, but my mum is dead. But God, I know that you love me. Thanks so much, God.

As with any lament, it ends with some words of encouragement. We may not have an influence on governmental decisions, but there is power in prayer. Our primary goal is fostering hope in those we serve.

Years later, I traveled to Uganda to offer workshops for both adults and children from a connection through my church. Heather, who is the daughter of my pastors, believes mental health is her God-given purpose and traveled with me to Uganda in 2014 after participating in a mental health workshop. Heather is a worshipper, well-balanced, wise and spiritually mature. Heather obtained an undergraduate degree in psychology, and I eagerly wait for her to resume mission projects in mental health when her children are older. Heather shares about her experience as part of the Uganda team.

> I was most impacted by my experience during training at a local church when Lyn began teaching on epilepsy. Suddenly we heard

a blood-curdling scream as Sarah (not her name) ran full-speed into the church, fell onto the dirt floor, and began convulsing.

Immediately, women from Sarah's community gathered around her, shouting prayers and cursing the spirit that caused her to seize. Lyn took charge in the most calm and gentle manner, rolled Sarah on her side so she wouldn't aspirate, and encouraged the friends to give her space. The episode soon subsided, and the woman fell asleep, exhausted from what her body had endured.

We learned from others that Sarah had these episodes regularly, and they believed she might be possessed by a spirit. In real time, Lyn was able to teach on epilepsy and other neurological conditions and give practical guidance on how the community should handle any seizure activity they may encounter in the future. Through this training, over thirty people gained knowledge, understanding, and compassion for others like Sarah. We could not have planned a better hands-on lesson.

I thought I was training under her in preparation for a trip to Uganda, but through her material I found I was also studying myself. I had many 'lightbulb moments' where things I learned from the material clicked into place with my own experiences and I understood myself and my past on a deeper level. Though the training material is extensive, these moments of insight continued to excite me and spur me on to continue learning.

Lyn has been a faithful friend and has always seen more in me than I see in myself. She has been a teacher, a listening ear, an encourager, and a prayer partner for me, and I am ever grateful for the time, insight, and wisdom she has chosen to invest in me.

Our team spent two weeks in Uganda and were deeply moved by responses from men and women on the topic of sexual assault. We chose to separate men and women. There were no men on our team, so Heather and the other team members met with the women, and I met with the men since I am an older woman, the psychologist, and an ordained minister.

The men blamed women for rape, stating it happened because they dressed inappropriately and went to unsafe areas. After I spent some time with the men, they learned that taking sex from someone without consent is assault. They realized their own responsibility. They asked forgiveness from the women on behalf of all men.

In response, the women extended forgiveness. They added, "We are not animals. We are not made of wood or iron. We are human beings." Both men and women spoke from the heart, and healing took place. Both groups listened to each other's stories. Deeper understanding and connectedness occurred.

I was profoundly impacted by the move of the Holy Spirit. When the men and I returned, the women were still in discussion, so the men prayed outside. After discussion, the women also began to pray. Open discussion coupled with prayer broke through layers and years of pain, misperceptions, and unforgiveness. Only God can move in such a dramatic way in so short a time. The woman's response that "we" are not animals, not made of wood or iron, but "we" are human beings reached deep into my own experience, applying the balm of Gilead to my own traumatic past. Healing continues, day by day, until we see Jesus when he takes away all pain.

Burundi

The project in Burundi was precipitated by an email from a pastor through Tributaries. Samuel and Soulé traveled to Burundi, but I chose not to join them since the travel route would have included driving through Rwanda with an overnight stay. I am willing to lose my life for the sake of the gospel, but only when I know the Holy Spirit goes before me. I did not have such assurance for the project in Burundi.

Dieudonne, the pastor who hosted the workshop, lost his wife a few weeks before the training. After the chapter on grief, he was able to speak of his pain, and other participants in the workshop were supportive. Before the training, cultural and religious beliefs led him to suffer silently. Dieudonne said:

> I was confused and hopeless. I felt humiliated and worthless, and I was jealous and uncomfortable to see other men enjoying being with their wives. I was against remarriage to the point that anyone who would talk to me about marriage was considered an enemy on the spot. When I learned about stress, grief, and trauma during the workshop, I started interacting with people again. Now I have remarried, and between my wife and I, we have eleven children. All of us are happy and doing well. I now teach about grief in the church and organize seminars for widows.

Both Samuel and Soulé have lost children and know deep pain. Though Jeff had a life-threatening illness, he did survive. I can't identify in the way Samuel and Soulé do with people who have lost a spouse or child. They have courageously walked through the journey of grief rather than skip over it, even though it's excruciatingly painful to do so.

Pastors who share their grief openly and genuinely give the congregation permission to share their pain. Some men will not cry, and in many cultures, they are not allowed to do so. We gently remind them Jesus wept. Being vulnerable and transparent offers an opportunity for people to join you in your grief.

Traveling on and between continents stirs a mixture of thoughts, feelings, and behavior. Many experiences are inspiring and encouraging, but on occasion there are unnecessary obstacles. A common obstacle is unnecessary inquiries and frequent delays either entering or exiting a country. Some officials (not the majority) are motivated by power or greed rather than by a motivation to maintain safe borders. Each situation is unique but typically occurs when I am extremely tired from extended travel or stressed by excessively hot temperatures. At times, I become discouraged.

Some days I wonder if I have the energy or the desire to wade through unnecessary inconveniences. The older I get, the more difficult travel becomes, and the more I need to care for myself as I care for others. New missionaries see the adventure but may not recognize that along with privilege comes sacrifice. And because missionaries tend to share the positive without the negative, it gives a false impression for those who come after us. Paul was honest about his struggles but said he had learned to be content in all circumstances. The one thing he chose to do is to forget what lies behind and instead pressed on to the high calling of Christ Jesus. I've learned to express my frustration, take a deep breath, and move forward.

Chapter Twenty-Eight

The Americas

The Americas not only cover a large geographical territory, but a broad range of cultures, languages, educational levels, spiritual diversity and low-high-income countries. In the Americas, I experience somewhat less stress since many people speak English as their first language, and travel time is often shorter. Long flights, jet lag, and time changes aren't quite as drastic and physically taxing as traveling to Asia or Africa. Projects have been offered in Ecuador, Peru, Mexico, and others.

All the mental health projects in South America have occurred by connections through missionaries in my church, other mental health professionals, and SEAPC. The mental health team supports several missionaries and is intentional about partnering together on different projects for kingdom purposes. Multiple languages are spoken, and Spanish and Portuguese are prevalent. The term Hispanic is used for countries that speak Spanish, but the term Latin America includes those speaking Portuguese and other languages.

Everything God creates is beautiful—South America is no exception. Cultures are vibrant, the music lively, and the dress is colorful. Church services fluctuate from reverent Catholic masses to exuberant Protestant singing and dancing. Both forms of worship please God and provide opportunities for people to spend time building their relationship with Jesus.

Ecuador

A project was planned for Ecuador in 2019. We drove from Guayaquil, at 13 feet elevation, to Cuenca, at 8,400 feet. We stopped for lunch, and experienced incredible views of dew-kissed mountains, meandering streams full of fish, and crisp air mingled with the fragrant foliage unfolding before us. A surprise was a glimpse of alpacas grazing in fields amidst Incan ruins in the middle of the city.

The project was implemented in connection with Unsion TV, the largest station broadcasting across Latin America. Unsion offers multiple resources for people near and far. One group provides general counseling services; another group, the April Project, focuses primarily on substance use problems and the complications they bring to relationships.

Some months after project completion, the leader reported continued change in both team health and individual counseling sessions.

> "Our search for the perfect material to train new counselors in the urban and rural communities of Ecuador has ended. This material is both a gift and a weapon when placed in the right hands. ... People are experiencing true freedom. Our team has found a new confidence and answers for the broken people of our city."

The team visited the Sanctuary of the Virgen del Rocio, which is built directly into the rock of the mountain. Much of its exterior is visible, a stunning white structure penetrating the expansive sky above. The rear wall is stone, and the vaulted ceilings and pipe organ drew us in to sit for a bit of the mass. The church was built in the 1880s, after the area had experienced a severe drought, and the townspeople wanted to honor God for answering their prayers for rain. Sitting in the presence of God in such a massive building emphasizes how deep and wide His love is for us.

Peru

The Tributaries team met Debora through a fellow missionary and short-term team member. Debora holds both Peruvian and Bolivian citizenship, which gives her a broader perspective on cultural differences across the continent. She came to visit our team in Virginia, and we made plans for a project in Cusco the following year. Five people were on the team, and I was the only one who did not speak Spanish. The compressed schedule created stress, but the participants actively participated, and we learned new things in the process.

No one has more energy, curiosity, or passion than Debora, and it was a delight to partner with her in Peru. Debora shared that the training has had a huge impact on her ministry to future generations and her ability to provide member care to partner church leaders. Debora shared a story about her work with children:

> As a teacher who ministers to K–12 school students and their parents who face daily challenges and struggles, I am blessed to guide them and refer them to health care workers for mental health treatment now that I have had training. A primary school student was suffering deep depression because he was not doing well at school, and he lacked social skills. The parents refused to accept that he had some learning disabilities, but mental health professionals confirmed he had autism spectrum disorder. Thank God he was able to receive specific help and extra support at school.
>
> The mental health training changed me personally, as I renewed my mindset about mental health care in the communities of faith and became more aware of what can help or harm the wellbeing of others. Now I have become a mental health advocate for kids and women in crisis to bring change in the communities of Peru and Bolivia.

Sandra, another close friend, has become a primary facilitator for a host of reasons. Not only is Sandra an excellent translator and interpreter, but she has stellar administrative and logistical skills. She shifts into overdrive when circumstances demand immediate attention and decreases my burden in the process. Born in Chile and with global travel experience, Sandra adapts to any environment with grace and fervent prayer. She has devoted her life as a wife, mother, missionary, and ordained minister for kingdom work. Sandra attended the mental health workshop in the US, then served with me in Peru and the Dominican Republic. Sandra shared that after the sudden loss of her husband Mark, attending the workshop contributed to a better understanding of the grief process, helped her understand that loss and trauma take time to heal, and gave her steps to take during her healing journey. Sandra said:

> In Cusco, participants shared stories about the general lack of knowledge about grief. One woman expressed her pain as she described unhelpful comments people made when her husband died. Some people don't know how to help and can cause more damage and hurt rather than bringing healing.

The team struggled during this project, as the altitude was over 11,000 feet. I admit it was a bit frightening for me to have a low oxygen level, palpitations, and difficulty breathing. My previous cardiac episode in 2007 added anxiety and concern that I might not be able to serve at higher elevations. Yet the team recovered, and not only training but also a team excursion was possible.

Machu Picchu is a fifteenth-century Inca citadel located at 7,970 feet elevation, significantly lower in elevation than Cusco, where the training was held. The team took a train through lush scenery, then hopped on the bus that takes visitors to the historical site. I was told the climb was easy, and a photo was possible very near where the bus dropped us off. I started the climb and became acutely aware that each historical site I climb gets more difficult as I age, and Machu Picchu is located at a higher elevation than most.

I made it up and then back down sixty-seven flights of steps to the bus stop, clearly due to my team members' help. If I had known ... Many times, after touring some amazing natural or manmade wonder of the world, I think, if I had known ... The initial climb was manageable; but the higher we went, the more difficult the steps were to navigate, and I repeatedly asked, "How much farther do we need to go?"

Irritated tour guides with other groups would reply, "It's just ahead."

Caleb, too, thought the promised land was just ahead. Though disappointed, he persevered patiently. Caleb's refusal to quit and dogged determination propel me forward when I want to go back.

Mexico

My ministry mandate requires that I travel to intensely dark places in the world to partner with Jesus to break spiritual chains and set people free. Ministry trips to Mexico, where there are strongholds of spiritism, trigger my vulnerabilities. The near kidnapping in 1990 left wounds and opened doors that are not completely healed. Face-to-face conflict with strongholds of voodoo or Santeria requires greater vigilance and powerful prayer coverage. I've made two ministry trips to Mexico since 1994; both trips were to attend SEAPC Friends Around the Table Prayer Conferences. My journeys in Mexico have been pits or wilderness, rather than mountaintop experiences. I understand how far I've come spiritually yet recognize that defeating strongholds occurs one day at a time.

My latest trip occurred near the end of October in 2024. I did not think about the timing of the conference until I entered the city and saw skeletons and other objects related to Dia de los Muertos, or Day of the Dead. I purposed to pray for people who needed release from bondage and chains broken. I prayed over the city, then prayed at the cathedral in the city center. I was impressed to pray for thousands trapped behind a wall who could not escape spiritual captivity. I was confident my prayers made a difference, and I went to bed at peace.

Soon after, however, I experienced night terrors. I knew the process would be grueling, and I wondered how long it would last. But this time I knew that Jesus would see me through to its perfect end as He has so many times in the past. I struggled for nearly twenty-four hours, and the Holy Spirit spoke to me constantly through Scriptures, songs, and creation. On departure, flying over Mexico City, I saw a volcano with smoke dramatically overpowering the atmosphere. I immediately considered Psalm 18:6-9, which describes David's cry for help from his strong enemies. The Lord heard him and expressed His anger through trembling mountains and smoke from His nostrils. God promises to save me from my enemies just as He did for David. My strength comes through God's grace.

I listened to sermons and worship songs on the drive from the airport. By the time I reached the house, I was free from torment but realized how complacent I had become toward the battle between good and evil. This was a wake-up call.

> But now, this is what the Lord says—he who created you, Jacob, he who formed you, Israel: "Do not fear, for I have redeemed you; I have summoned you by name; you are mine. When you pass through the waters, I will be with you; and when you pass through the rivers, they will not sweep over you When you walk through the fire, you will not be burned; the flames will not set you ablaze." (Isaiah 43:1-2)

Deuteronomy 7:22-23 declares that the journey is filled with giants (both natural and spiritual), or nations appearing to be greater than me.

> The Lord your God will drive out those nations before you, little by little. You will not be allowed to eliminate them all at once, or the wild animals will multiply around you. But the Lord your God will deliver them over to you, throwing them into great confusion until they are destroyed. (Deuteronomy 7:22-23)

I remembered a Scripture that has become pivotal for me. On an ordinary day in 2013, I read Psalm 118:12 from the English Standard Version. "They surrounded me like bees; they went out like a fire among thorns; in the name of the Lord, I cut them off." I was intrigued by the thought, and the Holy Spirit whispered, "Fire-quenching thorns." The Rhema word, or a word from God spoken at a specific moment in time, reached my innermost being and shared truth in a profound way.

Painting by Betty Nance Smith

The bees in this Scripture represent the sting of sins perpetrated against me as well as my own poor choices. Isaiah 9:18 reads, "Surely wickedness burns like a fire; it consumes briers and thorns, it sets the forest thickets ablaze, so that it rolls upward in a column of smoke."

Though wickedness burns like fire and consumes thorns, it cannot consume the crown of thorns Jesus wore—seemingly forced on Him by others, but by His own choice He carried the sin and the pain of others.

No plan, no power of the enemy can undo what Jesus provides through His blood. Wickedness destroys, but the crown of thorns gives life. To walk this road of life without Jesus leaves me powerless. To surrender to Him protects me through His blood, and I can then cut the enemy off in the name of the Lord.

Exodus 22:6 reads, "If a fire breaks out and spreads into thornbushes so that it burns shocks of grain or standing grain or the whole field, the one who started the fire must make restitution." The enemy of my soul consumed my life. I consumed my life. Since

Satan will not make restitution, and I cannot, Jesus paid the price in full. I live because Jesus died on the cross for me.

One day I was walking and worshipping with my arms outstretched. "Ouch!" I cried. I'd inadvertently stretched my arm out and was pierced by cactus needles. I remembered Jesus' outstretched arms, nailed to the cross, the crown of thorns on His head. My momentary sting, insignificant compared to His agony on the cross, was a bitter reminder of His sacrifice through crucifixion.

It reads in 1 Corinthians 15:54-55 that death has been swallowed up in victory, and the sting of death is sin. The realization that death has lost its sting profoundly alters my perspective. The past is over. I am no longer captive to past pain or past sin. And Jesus is no longer on the cross, wearing the crown of thorns. It is finished, and I am free. Having stood the test, I receive the crown of life the Lord promises to those who love Him. (James 1:12). The Lord of Lords reigns victorious, and I receive the benefit. Having spent more years loving Jesus than ignoring Him, I focus on what lies ahead and not on what has been.

My trip to Mexico thrust me into the swarm of fiery bees but also reminded me the "I AM" is immutable. My salvation comes from the blood of Jesus, who rules and reigns forever.

> With joy you will draw water from the wells of salvation. And you will say in that day: "Give thanks to the Lord, call upon his name, make known his deeds among the peoples, proclaim that his name is exalted. Sing praises to the Lord, for he has done gloriously; let this be made known in all the earth. Shout, and sing for joy, O inhabitant of Zion, for great in your midst is the Holy One of Israel." (Isaiah 12:3-6, ESV)

PART SIX.
NEARING THE SUMMIT

Chapter Twenty-Nine

Mountain Tales

Doors open on every continent. Global mental health projects increase my understanding of cultures, religions, people groups, and how my faith intersects with the faith of others. Walking their roads and climbing their mountains makes the experience real while giving me the privilege of praying with my feet on the ground. I've been given the rare gift to live life as a local and struggle with their day-to-day issues. Equally important, I have the opportunity to capture the unique beauty of world-famous cities adorned with towering buildings, or marvel at the simplicity of a small child pulling a Coke-can car by a string in a small village.

When Mercy Ships staff returned application photos of me and of Jeff from 1996, I paused to reflect. I had traveled to Mercy Ships with Jeff, in an old car, and with $500 per month when I was forty-five years old. I've pondered the complexities of life and the incredible privilege of sharing heartaches and victories with Jesus.

In 1991, I had wondered what I lived for, if my life made a difference. What was my purpose? I now know. My purpose is to share my faith and offer hope to desperate people, especially children. This may be through individual conversations or by training others to do the same. I have thousands of one-of-a-kind people in my head. Their stories remind me of the relationships I've made over the years, and how thankful I am to have people to share both the bitter and sweet experiences in our lives. Jesus knits us together through good times and bad times.

The conference speaker's words from 1996 remain true today: "You ask, when is it your turn? The time is now! I had to do some cutting away." My long-term missions journey began decades ago, but today is still my time, and God is still cutting away imperfections and hindrances. Cutting away is a lifelong process.

Some people suggest that it's time for me to fully retire, but that does not resonate with me. I remind myself that Caleb took the mountain at eighty-five years old, staring down giants as he climbed. I continue the climb, staring down my own giants. I may not be able to physically climb like Caleb, but I am well able to climb spiritual mountains of one sort or another until I take my last breath.

While I continue to offer mental health training, I'm handing over new content development and program expansion to others. Writing plays a bigger part as I age. I've now been writing for over a decade, but telling my story was harder than I expected. Fear of the unknown, fear of man, and fear of failure caused hesitation. I might be misunderstood. I might face rejection. Yet if I don't write, I miss an opportunity to inspire and encourage others; to share a singular story of the joys and sorrows, natural and spiritual battles experienced by serving in long-term missions. Most importantly, desperate people might not learn that their future can be brighter than their past. I choose to write, daring to live on the edge yet again.

Daring to live on the edge frightens many. Predictability, consistency, standing still, offer many the illusion of security. Yet Helen Keller wrote, "Security is mostly a superstition. It does not exist in nature, nor do the children of men as a whole experience it. Avoiding danger is no safer in the long run than outright exposure. Life is either a daring adventure, or nothing." Yes, there is no security in the natural world. I'd rather live on the edge and trust God for dream fulfillment than stand on the sidelines wondering what I'm missing.

Before the first keystroke, I remembered a book I had read as a child. *Hitty: Her First Hundred Years* is the tale of a carved wooden doll, created to ward off evil, told from the doll's point of view. Hitty experienced abandonment and rejection, became a pincushion, was a "throw away" doll, then was stolen by bullies in the night. Many of her stories paralleled my own.

Hitty changed over time. Initially, she was terrified when calamity struck. But eventually, she learned to look not only at the problem but at the beauty of her surroundings. She grew stronger as she weathered difficulties, and her perspective changed. I've grown stronger and changed as well.

Hitty is sold at auction, a horrifying experience during which she was powerless. Two people purposed to have her, with clashing motives. The first, a loud, aggressive woman, reminded her of the chief of the foreign tribespeople. She wanted possession. The other, a kind, fatherly man, softly countered every offer. He wanted relationship. The bidding started. "Fifty dollars!" the brash woman shrieked. The woman walked off, confident of her purchase, of her victory. Hitty writes, "But before the last blow of the hammer, the gentle man beneath the pine tree said, 'Fifty-one dollars,' and I knew that I was saved."

Like Hitty, my story does not end with darkness and broken promises. Jesus waited for me as I trudged through the shadow of death and wooed me with the prayer of St. Francis. His Light effortlessly drew me close. He loves me. He never leaves me or forsakes me. I am His.

Acknowledgements

Special thanks to Jeff Dahl, my amazing son and creative editor; Kay Helm, copyeditor; Georges Mbeck, interior design; and Betty Nance Smith, who painted the illustration of fire-quenching thorns. Endorsement by Deyon Stephens.

Reviewers: Don and Deyon Stephens; Ken Cramer; Amy Curtis; Matt Geppert; Wayna Lamar; Karen Lea; Donna Mills; and Laurel Houck.

Long- and short-term team members, family, friends, financial and prayer supporters for over 30 years. This is your story, too.

About the Author

Dr. Lyn Westman is director of the mental health pillar at LightHouse Church in Hayes, Virginia, and the former Mental Health Program Consultant for both Mercy Ships and Tributaries International. Lyn designs and implements mental health and trauma healing training programs globally, training formal and informal care providers from a holistic perspective. She has worked internationally since 1980.

Lyn is the author of *Understanding People, Mental Health, and Trauma*, a mental health training manual. In 2015, she wrote *Baby Finds Grace* to bring healing to people, especially children who suffer from stress, grief and/or trauma. She is a coauthor of *Bringing Healing to Children*.

Lyn is an ordained minister. She earned a Ph.D. in Psychology from United States International University (now Alliant University) in 1995, and a Master of Psychiatric Nursing from the University of California at Los Angeles in 1980.

Notes

1. The song is "Brightest and Best of the Stars of the Morning," lyrics by Reginald Heber, from *The Christian Observer* (1811).

2. Lee Webber, "Crossings" Cited in Parables, etc. *Guideposts,* November 1986, Vol. 6, 3.

3. Johanna Mcgeary and Marguerite Michaels, "Africa Rising," *TIME,* March 30, 1998, https://time.com/archive/6732494/africa-rising-3/

4. Deepa Lama, Keshar, "Nabolau Malai Paagal Bhani," Translated lyrics provided by KOSHISH Nepal. (April 18, 2016), Video, 3:59, https://www.youtube.com/watch?v=Mm941c52tDs

Abbreviations

AMPC	Amplified Bible, Classic Edition
BFG	Baby Finds Grace
DRC	Democratic Republic of the Congo
DTS	Discipleship Training School
ELWA	Eternal Love Winning Africa
ESV	English Standard Version
FGM	Female genital mutilation
GRASP	Global Relief Action for Social Protection
HCS	Health Care Services
IMF	International Ministerial Fellowship
JAV	Journey Against Violence
LRA	Lord's Resistance Army
mhGAP-IG	The Mental Health Gap Intervention Guide
NGO	Non-governmental organization
SEAPC	Southeast Asia Prayer Center
SIL	Summer Institute of Linguistics
TILTI	The International Leadership Training Institute
UNMIL	United Nations Military
UPMHT	Understanding People, Mental Health and Trauma
WHO	World Health Organization
YFC	Youth for Christ
YWAM	Youth With A Mission

Made in the USA
Coppell, TX
28 January 2026